It Was Me All Along?

**CULTIVATE HAPPINESS
THROUGH MINDFUL AWARENESS**

Rita Louise, PhD

Copyright © 2024 by SoulHealer Press

No part of this book may be reproduced or utilized in any form or by any means: electronic, mechanical or otherwise, including photocopying, recording or by any informational storage and retrieval system without permission in writing from the author.

Although the author has researched all sources to ensure the accuracy and completeness of the information contained within this book, no responsibility is assumed for errors, inaccuracies, omissions, or inconsistency herein. Any slights of people, places or organizations are completely and totally unintentional.

ISBN # 978-0-9758649-3-7 Print

ISBN # 978-0-9758649-4-4 Ebook

Library of Congress Control Number: 2023921197

First Edition

Printed Marshall, TX, USA

Screw everyone else, this book is dedicated to me. Why? Because I've worked hard and want to acknowledge the profound changes I have made in myself and my life. Yea me! In the immortal words of Toby Keith,

"How do you like me now?"

Acknowledgements

There are so many people that I want to offer my sincere gratitude. To the people who allowed me to experience their awesome, healthy, healing, high vibration, thank you for being you. I love you to the moon and back.

I also want to acknowledge the individuals who created chaos in my inner world and interfered with my groove. You caused me to stop, check in and decide if I wanted you in my life. Thank you for helping me learn discernment. Sorry, you have to go now.

A sincere thanks to Kristy Lemmon and her Gentle Flow Yoga classes. Even on days when I would find myself upset, cranky or just out of it, she always created a space where I could focus on my breathing while practicing being mindfully aware. This allowed me realign my energy, reset my inner world and find my Zen. Ahhhh….

Last but not least, to Debbie Adams Gullett for laughing at my bad jokes and talking me down when I had bad brain. Thank you for your unwavering support as I went through the paces of finding myself.

Contents

INTRODUCTION	1
OUR MYSTERIOUS INNER WORLD	11
THE MAKE-UP OF OUR MIND	18
The Conscious Mind	19
Thoughts & The Thought Processes	19
An Unsettling Fact	22
Intrusive Thoughts	23
THE SUBCONSCIOUS MIND	26
The Nature Of The Subconscious Mind	27
ME AND MY EMOTIONS	37
EMOTIONS AND EMOTIONAL REGULATION	41
FIGHT, FLIGHT, FREEZE, FAWN	43
The Fight Stress Response	44
The Flight Stress Response	45
The Freeze Stress Response	46
The Fawn Response	50
EMOTIONAL ADDICTION	52
It's All About The Chemistry	57
THE SELF-AWARENESS GAME	63
SELF-AWARENESS	65
Mindfulness	66
New Mantra For Living	69
YOUR INNER WORLD AWAITS	71
The Science Of Breathing	73
Working With The Breath	74

 Trying Mindfulness On For Size 79
 Asking Questions 85

THE COURAGE TO CHANGE 91

 IDENTIFYING OUR STUFF 95
 EMOTIONAL AWARENESS 98
  Noticing And Naming our Emotions 99
  Growing Your Emotional Awareness 102
 OBSERVING OUR BEHAVIORS 107
  The Power Of Choice 108
  Akrasia And Enkrateia 110
  Making Lasting Behavioral Changes 112
  An Exercise For My Procrastinator Friends 120
 CHANGING OUR AUTOMATIC THOUGHTS 121
  The 17-Second Rule 122
  Challenging Your Inner Critic 124
  I Am! 125
  Digging To The Core 127
  Putting Our Stories To Rest 130
  Quit Your Kvetching 133

THE SUPERCONSCIOUS MIND 139

 THE SPIRIT IN THE SKY 144
 THE SOUL 146
  The Devolution Of The Soul 147
  The Battle For Your Soul 149
 OUR HIGHER SELF 151
  What It Feels Like To Receive A Message 152
  Inspired Action 154
 OUR INDELIBLE SPIRIT 157
  Going With The Flow 159

OH NO! NOT POSITIVE EMOTIONS! 163

 MOVING UP THE SCALE OF POSITIVE EMOTIONS 166
 ROADMAP TO OUR EMOTIONS 172
  Feeling The Shift 173

THE GAME OF LIFE AND HOW TO PLAY IT 177

The Law Of Attraction 183
The Fine Print *186*
Instant Karma *188*
A Soapbox Moment *189*

PEOPLE, NOT PEOPLE 193

The Law Of Resonance 195
Fine-Tuning Our Awareness 198
The Dreaded B Word 204
Why Communication Matters *207*
Wanting Them To Change *209*
But I Don't Want To *211*
Purgatory 214
Emotional Neutrality *216*

FINAL, FINAL THOUGHTS 221

Introduction

"You are being presented with a choice: evolve or remain. If you choose to remain unchanged, you will be presented with the same challenges, the same routines, the same storms, the same situations until you learn from them, until you love yourself enough to say "no more."

– Craig Crippen

Did you read my last book, *The Dysfunctional Dance of the Empath and Narcissist?* You might recall the text opened with the shocking realization that most of my relationships, especially my romantic ones, were formed with self-serving, self-absorbed men. Yes, they were narcissists. I, at the time, was sad and confused. Why did I keep attracting toxic people into my life? I came to grasp that my pattern of participating in unhealthy associations originated in my youth. The cause: the dysfunctional family environment I was raised in.

I was determined to learn all I could about childhood trauma and how it affected me as an adult. I wanted to change whatever kept landing me in these situations. More importantly, I never wanted to return to the arms of an abuser. I was tired of failed relationships and hurting inside. I wanted to be with someone who didn't just think about himself, his needs, and his desires while discounting mine. I felt deep down there would be a rainbow at the end of this tunnel once I figured it out, so I set off to work.

This began my journey to comprehend, uncover and heal what had controlled my life and my relationships. I knew a part of my healing process was to write a book outlining my findings. I felt my research and its subsequent publication could offer my fellow empaths, codependents, and the chronic fawners of the world the insights and tools needed to create real and lasting changes in their lives. Perhaps they could also break free from ongoing cycles of maltreatment.

I was in the process of finalizing *The Dysfunctional Dance* when I entered into a new relationship. I believed I had solved all of my bad relationship choices. I knew what to look for and felt confident I would not settle for another unhealthy situation. I was going to put my recent learnings to the test.

My new beau appeared emotionally secure, supportive, kind, and loving. I felt safe and nurtured. It was everything I was hoping for. I was able to open up and be completely vulnerable with him. I have never cried so much in front of another human being in my life. I knew I had a safe place to land regardless of what was happening to me. The relationship was refreshing and unlike anything I had experienced in the past.

Well, I will be the first to admit it. I miscalculated the steps necessary to eradicate oneself from the dysfunctional dance. My hope for a happily ever after wasn't happy. Thankfully, it didn't last forever.

Part of me would love to share all the gory details about this relationship flop, but something else contributed to the profound revelations that later emerged. My work, my business of 30 years, was failing amid the Covid pandemic and the forced lockdowns. I did everything I could think of to revive it. Regardless of what I tried, nothing worked. I watched my savings start to dwindle, which brought up a tremendous fear within me, the fear that I would be destitute and not survive.

I was becoming increasingly desperate regarding my financial predicament. I was running around like a chicken with its head cut off. I was working on overdrive, trying anything and everything to regroup. In the end, I had a tough decision to make. Do I throw in the towel and give up? Do I walk away from a lifetime of work and get a regular job to make ends meet? I was at a loss. I was mentally and emotionally exhausted trying to figure it all out.

Then I started to get sick. I was coughing all of the time. I was having difficulty breathing, and at times my chest would hurt. This added to the terror I was feeling. What if something was really wrong with me? What would I do? How would I take care of myself?

I finally broke down and asked 'Mr. Right' for help. We were living together, and I paid all the essential household bills. He would emphatically state in the midst of all of this, I didn't need to get a traditional job. He let me pointedly know if things got really bad, we could easily live on his retirement salary. I decided to take him up on his offer. I prayed his financial support would take some of the pressure off of me.

All I wanted was for him to buy groceries. After a very uncomfortable and triggering one-way conversation, I was offered $100 a month as his contribution to the household expenses. His level of indifference to the overpowering alarm I was feeling was deplorable. What happened to *"We can live on my retirement?"*

I felt even more alone than I had before. When my plea for a lifeline was summarily dismissed, I was thrown into the depths of depression and started having panic attacks. It robbed me of the last bit of hope I had. Thankfully, the relationship ended not long after. I had nothing to lose at that point, which included him.

Something fascinating happened two days after his departure. All the symptoms I experienced, the coughing, the chest pain, and trouble breathing miraculously disappeared. Hmmmm……

I was forced to start the process of rebuilding not just my hurt feelings but my whole life. I no longer had my work as a refuge to mask my emotional pain. I had nothing, or it seemed like nothing at the time. It took every bit of my energy to forge some level of hope that things would turn around and start moving forward again.

The anguish I was experiencing caused me to look in the mirror and say, *"No More!"* I couldn't do this to myself again. I could no longer allow myself to be hurt, mistreated, ignored, minimized, or shunned by anyone ever again, especially by a man who professes his undying love for me.

It is often during times of our most profound hurt, our most significant transitions, that true healing is possible. It forces us to face our demons and look at ourselves with complete and brutal honesty. Many times these insights can be initially challenging to hear. However, if you pay attention and begin to act on them, you automatically open the door for forming long termed profound changes. Sarcastically speaking, I was thrilled to be back in this position again.

In light of my recent surprise, it seemed apparent that I had only scratched the surface of my recovery. This is not to discount any of the information provided in *The Dysfunctional Dance* as being somehow off base or faulty. What was discussed still holds true and needs to be addressed, acknowledged, and potentially acted on, particularly if you consistently attract toxic partners.

People have suggested over the years that I can be a bit hardheaded. Apparently, it required taking everything away from me, threatening me, my world, my very survival, for me to be beaten down enough to get the message and decide to change, although the jury is still out on that one.

I realized regardless of what I went through, there was one common denominator – 'Me.' I had to step back and look at my flaws - again. I could no longer point a finger at him, whoever he was at the moment. I was forced to accept responsibility for what I did or chose not to do. I have to tell you, it was a hard pill to swallow.

There were several issues I had to take stock of and well own. Even writing and putting these words on paper to share with you makes me cringe. I had to face the fact that I had some codependency issues to deal with. I could see the dots connecting the definition of this behavior and my own. But how could that be? I thought being codependent meant you were a people pleaser. I am not a people pleaser, I swear!!!

This concept all came crashing in one day. I was listening to a video by life coach Lisa Romano on YouTube where she talked about codependency. She explained that it is not uncommon for an emotionally healthy person to become involved with a narcissist. The difference, she stated, between a relationship with an emotionally healthy individual and a narcissist and someone who is codependent is that the healthy person will leave early on. They communicate their needs and desires, have boundaries, and have the courage to walk away if required. The wounded individual, on the other hand, will stay long after the relationship's expiration date. Okay, me again.

I concluded being concerned for the well-being of another was ingrained in me. I thought loving someone meant ensuring their needs were taken care of. I assumed they would do the same for me, and we would live some kind of a kumbaya life together. Isn't that how you 'do' relationships? From what I gather, the answer is *"No."*

I remember thinking, *"Well, how the hell do I change that?"* I then internalized a couple of questions that are the bane of any codependent's existence, *"What do I want?"* and *"What do I need?"* Embarrassing as this is to say, I really didn't know. To be honest, I never thought to ask. After some soul-searching, I came up with a few preliminary ideas.

I wanted to feel safe. I wanted to be happy. I was tired of feeling miserable inside and wanted to experience a sense of inner peace. Most importantly, I wanted to put all this relationship turmoil behind me. Was it possible? I had no idea. Being a consummate researcher and hardheaded, I set my sights on figuring this out, just as I had done in *The Dysfunctional Dance*. I hoped this new endeavor would finally solve my relationship problems and bring about world peace. Hey, it could happen.

This time, in place of trying to figure out 'Mr. Right' and the telltale signs of a detrimental relationship, the focus had to be on me. I needed to travel inward to the core of my being instead of looking at the outward expression of my trauma and dysfunction. I had to explore my inner world. I was all about it if it could somehow be changed, modified, or adjusted.

I have always considered myself a person of integrity. This is most evident in my business and intuitive counseling practice. I will say what needs to be said, no holds barred. Yet my inner world was not so clean cut. It triggered quickly, was too accepting of people's unacceptable behaviors, and was way too afraid to say something when a boundary was crossed.

As I began delving into my inner world, I discovered there was not just the confident, outgoing Dr. Rita inside. There was also Little Rita, a scared and traumatized 3-year-old who also inhabited this inner realm. She was sweet, innocent, silly, and very trusting. She just wanted one thing, to be loved by someone, anyone. Little Rita was afraid to exert herself for fear of negative consequences. She was willing to accept less-than-desirable situations versus expressing what she wanted or needed. Bottom line, Little Rita learned to tolerate a lot of crap and saw it as her lot in life.

From what I gathered, Little Rita was always hiding out in the shadows. This aspect of my personality always seemed to come forward in my close and especially in my romantic relationships. I loved the joy, playfulness, and big bright, excited smile she would bring to the table. I loved that part of myself. I felt alive when she was in play.

Okay, so I am not a psychopath with multiple personalities. We all have parts of ourselves we may or may not be aware of. Some people call these aspects our 'shadow self.' According to Carl Jung, the shadow self are traits we perceive as being negative or unacceptable to others, which we repress for fear of negative feedback. Over time, these suppressed feelings can become so deeply buried in our psyche that we have no notion of their existence.

One thing I read early in this exploration of my new life was all of this could be changed. I could find happiness and inner peace. Little Rita wasn't too sure about this whole prospect. It is interesting because much of what I will share on the pages that follow Dr. Rita already knew. She has utilized many of the concepts we will discuss at various times in her life, although not consistently. Dr. Rita is well aware of her inner world. She knows what she wants and needs to do.

She readily recognizes that the insights she receives, her spiritual steering, so to speak, actively guides her along her path. She relishes her relationship with spirit, God, the universe, source, or whatever name you want to put on it. Through a lifetime of hardheaded spiritual ass-kicking, she has learned to follow the dictates this unknown resource provides.

On the other hand, Little Rita hardly ever listens to this inner wisdom. And I have to tell you, the guidance she has received over the years did not come through as a soft, quiet whisper inside. There were many instances, especially in her close relationships, where it came through in a loud booming voice that would keep her up at night. Did she listen? No. She just accepted the discomfort. These feelings were normal to her and did not call for investigation or alarm.

Sadly, it never occurred to Little Rita to pay attention to her inner world. Usually, if something emotionally upsetting happened, she immediately dissociated and would be trapped in the freeze response. She didn't know things could be different, and the thought of happiness was unimaginable.

Then something happened. Little Rita discovered she had a choice. If she didn't like something or didn't want to do something, she could say *"No!"* If she felt hurt by someone's bad behavior, she could walk away and never return. Really? Really?

To an outsider, this may seem so basic, but to Little Rita, it was as if the secrets of the universe were revealed. You don't know how happy this made her feel. Now, to figure out how to do it and this is where our story begins.

How do you navigate your inner world? Are there things you can do, items to look out for, red flags to be had? I wanted to learn how to not be a codependent doormat any longer. How do I master being less accepting of others and more proactive about myself, my needs, and my desires, especially in the face of negativity? I guess we will find out together.

Dang! It Was Me All Along? is not about fixing your past. It is about looking inside and owning your thoughts, feelings, and emotions, and acting on them. Is it scary? Hell yea! Especially if you came from a toxic upbringing, are codependent, or are challenged with other limiting beliefs. Nevertheless, there is no way to move forward without throwing down the gauntlet and saying, *"This is what I want!"* and then going for it.

Please join me, Dr. Rita, and Little Rita on this path to a deeper level of healing. Imagine having permission to be happy. Imagine having it be okay to really enjoy your life. Imagine being free of inner conflict and second-guessing yourself. Imagine having the autonomy to decide who you are and how you want to interact with others.

Yes, you can choose! You can decide to take your life back. You can begin right here, right now. Grab my preverbal hand, and we will head out together on this glorious adventure. You have nothing to lose and everything to gain.

How To Use This Book

Dang! It Was Me All Along? is a journey, a journey into the heart of your very being. It contains thought provoking ideas that may challenge your way of viewing your life and your reality. It provides an image, a wide angle view of what is going on inside, insights that are not readily observable, that is unless you look.

You may see areas in your life where you excel. You might also uncover the parts of you that may need some of your time and attention. Specifically designed exercises are interspersed throughout to help you transcend harmful past programming or difficult life experiences, and bring you closer to the life you have been praying for.

My guidance for its use is simple. Read through the text fully and reflect on how it may relate to your life. Perhaps try and exercise or two along the way and then read it again. It is only by taking into consideration the big picture, the whole enchilada, as they say that you will find value in the guidance offered.

With the goal in hand you might be enticed to explore the exercises more fully and begin incorporating them into your daily life. You might not believe me right now, but this work will naturally lead you to an increasingly content, joyful and happy life.

Our Mysterious Inner World

"Be the silent watcher of your thoughts and behavior. You are beneath the thinker. You are the stillness beneath the mental noise. You are the love and joy beneath the pain."
— Eckhart Tolle

Let's face it. We don't pay attention to what is going on inside. We are taught to believe what is happening around us is more important than what is transpiring within. Our view of the world is often based on what we can see, hear, smell, taste, and touch. These external events are transformed within us into our thoughts, ideas, opinions, impressions, judgments, conclusions, their associated emotional responses, and our subsequent behaviors.

Our relationship with ourselves causes many of us to live in an anxious, neurotic, or hypervigilant state. We accept our internal discord as being normal. Life is one giant crapshoot. We find ourselves at the whim of everyone and everything we come upon. We are constantly being tossed around inside, our emotions going quickly from one to another. We endlessly ride the turbulent waves of highs and lows and are thankful for the periods of smooth sailing we occasionally encounter. That is, until the next storm strikes.

As we go through these seasons of chaotic ups and downs, we don't realize it can be different; we can be different. We accept the strong winds and the crashing waves. We pray, while in the thick of it, we do not go down with the ship. But what if you could learn to calm the sea, tame the winds, and navigate life full steam ahead?

I wouldn't have believed it if you suggested this to me a few years ago. I could not image my inner world being somehow different. The concept was foreign. It was an inalienable part of me, just like my sex, skin color, and race. As Popeye the Sailor would say, *"I am what I am."* I had come to accept this eternal, unchangeable part of myself.

My typical 'MO' (modus operandi) looked something like this. Something upsetting would happen, and I would have an emotional reaction. The adverse situation would put me into a cycle of negative thinking. Then I would start replaying the event in vivid detail over and over and over again in my mind. This would send me spiraling down a giant rabbit hole of negative thoughts.

I was very familiar with my rabbit hole. It was like being sent to my room, except this space exists in my mind, in my inner world. The hole wasn't well decorated, but you would think it held the secret elixir of life, considering how much time I would spend there. It was not unheard of for me to find myself trapped there for days and frequently weeks at a time. I guess I relished my negative thoughts even though they were painful and ultimately unhealthy. Heck, I didn't know any better.

Do you go down your own rabbit hole? Do you find that you constantly battle worry, anger, frustration, or fear? If this is you, taking control of what is happening inside can change, well, everything.

You might wonder, *"What the heck is this inner world?"* Simply put, our inner world is an intangible part of ourselves, yet it is no less real than our fingers and toes. It comprises a vast landscape filled with our thoughts, feelings, emotions, desires, dreams, hopes, and fears.

We are all aware of it on some level, but our inner world is like a well-guarded secret. People don't talk about it. They don't describe it or tell us how to operate it. And more importantly, they never let us in on the fact that it can be modified. We are left to our own devices, and maybe, just maybe, we will figure it out. If we only came with a road map, a user's manual, a secret decoder ring, or a step-by-step guide to point us in the right direction.

The quest to understand, navigate and transform this innate part of ourselves is the foundation of every wisdom tradition around the world. Practitioners of this occulted knowledge became skilled at regulating their conscious state of being. The insights they possessed, their 'how to' book, so to speak, was shrouded in secrecy and only passed on to select initiated individuals.

Garnering an understanding of our inner world is more attainable than it was in the past. The untellable mysteries of a bygone era have been revealed in modern years. In fact, many of the topics we will be exploring may seem familiar, although you may have yet to investigate them in any depth. The concepts come from fields including psychology, personal growth, religion, spirituality, biology, quantum physics, energy medicine, mindfulness, the Law of Attraction, and just plain common sense.

Don't worry. You do not need an advanced degree or an intrinsic understanding of arcane knowledge to comprehend the topic at hand. It also doesn't require that you hold any specific religious beliefs. Changing who you are, shifting your consciousness, and modifying your inner reality has nothing to do with a particular creed but instead necessitates a desire to transform yourself and your everyday experience.

My Mystery Date

Who we are and how we relate to the world is based upon an accumulation of thoughts we pick up over time. They work as a lens that shapes our reality. We can see victory and success ahead of us, or we can accept the agony of defeat long before we begin an endeavor.

We are fundamentally passive recipients of other people's opinions up until the age of seven, according to cell biologist Dr. Bruce Lipton. We are an amenable conduit, accepting what we see and hear as being true and factual. Then we adjust ourselves to fit the indoctrination we receive, which controls our decisions later in life.

Some of the programming we accept is wonderful, helpful, and supportive. It can cause us to have confidence in ourselves, work hard, and excel in life. Then there is the programming that can cripple us, make us think we are less than or as if something is wrong with us. This indoctrination influences our character, how we see ourselves, and how we view the world.

In the '60s, Milton Bradley released a game called *"Mystery Date."* The game's objective was to get matched up with one of the five possible men hidden behind a little plastic door. There was the 'formal dance' date, the 'bowling' date, the 'beach' date, the 'skiing' date, and the 'dud.' You had to start over if you, unfortunately, revealed the poorly dressed, unshaven man, the dud.

I enjoyed playing this game with my sister and her friends. I recall wondering if I would end up with the dud when I married. Even at my young age, I didn't think I deserved better. I could never see myself finding romantic bliss with the formal dance date, the man in the tuxedo carrying a bouquet of flowers.

One bit of programming I took on was delivered by my Uncle Jerry. For as long as I can remember, whenever I saw him, he would call me 'funny looking.' I would hear his words resonating in my mind whenever I peered into a mirror. I came to believe I must have been hideous since he repeatedly reminded me of my unfavorable appearance. While I now know he was only speaking in jest, I still have lingering doubts about my looks. Was that the reason I kept getting into relationships with duds?

It is not only someone's opinion about how you look that can distort what you think about yourself. You might have been told you weren't good at sports; you sang off-key, were dumb, or were not artistic. These little nuggets of unwanted, unsolicited, and hurtful information formed the foundation of your belief system.

Perhaps, because of it, you decided to never compete in sports again. Maybe you stopped singing in public, stopped trying hard in school, quit drawing or painting all because of what someone said. Add to it the cultural, political, and social economic beliefs we are all exposed to. They also play a role in sculpting our character.

Adults have better control over the data they take on. They have more life experience, a greater capacity to reflect on what happens, and are more readily equipped to discern fact from fiction. But sometimes, our life experiences are not so easily shaken off. People who find they are repeatedly getting let go from jobs, are consistently discarded in their relationships, and are overlooked, ignored, criticized, blamed, or overruled can begin to doubt themselves and their abilities.

So the question is: are you happy, content, and experiencing inner peace as you make it through your day? Alternatively, do you feel unhappy, hopeless, miserable, afraid, or suffering as you navigate life? Instead of focusing on having a relationship with a partner or mate, maybe you should explore having a relationship with yourself.

What would it be like to date yourself? Even the thought of it might bring up the inner commentary, *"Well, I don't even like her!"* Imagine getting to know how you operate. Envision discovering what you want, what you think, what you need, and what you desire and having it matter! Picture liking yourself, maybe even loving yourself!

Don't worry. This budding romance doesn't require you to buy expensive equipment, do sit-ups, push-ups, or squats. You don't have to buy new clothes, change your hairstyle or lose weight.

You don't even have to leave the comfort of your home if you don't want to.

What it does require is being open to developing an awareness of what is happening inside. You must be willing to access the furtive and sometimes scary places within yourself you may have avoided for years. Changing your inner landscape takes time and practice as you learn to fine-tune it. Once mastered, you might find the happily ever after you have been looking for.

When I started down the conscious path to inner awareness, I thought it would bring up all kinds of past trauma. Surprisingly this was not the case. I discovered reading books on healing trust, codependency, and developing boundaries in an attempt to fix myself was more upsetting than where we will be venturing. We are taking the path of love, not as in loving a partner but loving ourselves. So please take a deep breath as we open the door to your inner world and look around.

The Make-up Of Our Mind

Our mind is very complex, much more complex than we give it credit for. Most people don't understand its unique parts and how they function. Our mind consists of a variety of intricate layers, with our conscious mind forming a narrow window within its entirety. Outside this window lies the subconscious mind, the storehouse of our perceptions. It also contains a part of us that allows us to connect to higher states of being, our superconscious mind,

Nature holds many examples which exemplify our range of consciousness. Visible light, the light we can see with our naked eyes, for example, forms a small portion of the electromagnetic spectrum. The human eye can detect wavelengths between 400 nanometers (violet) to 700 nanometers (red). To the right of the visible spectrum, we find lower-frequency light waves, including infrared radiation, microwaves, and radio waves. We have ultraviolet (UV) rays, X-rays, and gamma rays to the left of the visible spectrum.

We find a similar thing occurring within us. There is our conscious mind, the part we are mentally aware of, the lower vibrating subconscious mind and the higher vibrating superconscious mind. We will break down each component part, investigating how they operate and explore ways to shift, change and transform them in order to create the best version of ourselves.

The Conscious Mind

The conscious mind is a great tool we have at our disposal. It is filled with an array of the thoughts, memories, and ideas we are cognizant of. One of its jobs is to observe and categorize what is happening around us. This helps simplify our decision-making process. The conscious mind is logical and analytical. We use it to think, assess, plan, remember, rehash, anticipate, compare, and figure things out. This allows us to quickly weigh possible consequences and predict the outcome of an event.

Our conscious awareness represents only a tiny portion of the workings of in our inner world. We only become aware of our mental processes when they enter the conscious mind. Surprisingly, we only use our conscious cognitive processing about 5% of the time. The remaining 95% of what is happening inside occurs outside our awareness.

Thoughts & The Thought Processes

Our thoughts are the primary feature of the conscious mind. They determine everything we do. They frame our world, inspire emotional reactions and our successive behaviors, yet we rarely think about thinking. Thoughts are often viewed as involuntary and automatic bodily functions like breathing, but they do not have to be.

Most people's minds are filled with a never-ending stream of thoughts. We have over 6,000 thoughts per day, according to a recent study conducted at Queen's University in Kingston, Ontario. A constant chatter is often happening inside our heads that begins when we wake up in the morning and doesn't stop until we fall asleep at night. Even when we are not conscious of thinking, we are still thinking.

Our thoughts typically gravitate to whatever is going on around us. Whatever we are giving our attention to activates a thought in our mind, both positive and negative. There might be times when we can focus our minds on one subject. Most of the time our thoughts shift and change without warning.

We might be thinking about what to have for dinner. In the next moment, we might find ourselves reminiscing about a friend. Then we're off to work where we are solving a problem, and in a flash, we're back to thinking about dinner again.

We can only accommodate one active thought in our conscious awareness at any given moment. When we shift our focus to something else, this becomes our active thought. This new thought fills the one awareness slot in our conscious mind deactivating the last one we had. We can think about the concert we will be going to with friends, or we can think about our cat as they walk across the room, but we cannot think of both of them at the same time.

Thoughts & Neural Pathways

Let's take this one step further. Our thoughts deepen through repetition. Every time we have a new idea, a fresh neural pathway forms. When we bring forth the same thought down the road, it is easier for us to experience it. These newly formed neural pathways start as the road less traveled. They become bigger, wider, more dominant, increasingly entrenched, and embedded in our psyche the more we indulge them.

Well-worn neural pathways are readily seen in our kneejerk reactions. The thought, idea, or concept becomes second nature to us. Where our mind reflexively goes indicates the size and strength of one neural pathway over another. We do not have to think about 'it' any longer. Our body and conscious mind will automatically 'go there' to the places where we have spent the most time laying down progressively stronger neural pathways.

Our prevailing neural pathways influence our mindset. They can cause us to see what we wish to see, abundance or lack-there-of, safety or danger, pleasure or punishment. They put a magnifying glass on specific attributes while disregarding the rest.

I grew up in a family of negative thinkers. My Dad always saw life through a half-full cup. Actually, his cup was always empty, but that is another story. He always found something to complain about it in every encounter. It is called 'kvetching' in Yiddish. My Dad was a consummate, professional 'kvetcher.' I'm not sure he would have much to say if there wasn't something to gripe about.

Years ago, my parents went to a family friend's wedding. A string quartette played in the background as they dined on lobster thermidor. There was a live band, which entertained the guests after the meal.

I do not know what other marvels this event held, but my Dad's assessment of the nuptials was *"the food was cold."* He was also aghast at the price tag. They had paid over $40,000 for the shindig. That was all he could see and ultimately tell us about the festivities.

Some people's active neural pathways automatically take them to a place of peace, understanding, satisfaction, happiness, or awe, regardless of the situation. For others, a happenstance can quickly take them to the dark side. They might reactively feel fearful, angry, frustrated, pessimistic, or hopeless. They may constantly complain, seeing only lack, loss, or rejection. They may only remember the bad times and never the good. Feelings of joy and gratitude are not in their vocabulary or way of thinking.

An Unsettling Fact

A National Science Foundation research study offers a startling fact about our thoughts. They concluded about 80% of our thinking is negative. This means that 80% of the time, we are worried, anxious, in fear, or are trapped in regret or blame. The unsettled nature of our mind means we can go from nervous to fearful to being filled with dread in the blink of an eye.

One negative thought can set off a cascade of undesirable thinking, with one leading to the emergence of another and then another. They can branch out from our initial notion until we are bombarded with a torrent of semi-related ideas.

In addition, the study revealed about 95% of our thoughts are repetitive. This is most readily seen when we are having one of those days. Perhaps you were visiting your rabbit hole or were lying in bed trying to sleep but couldn't shut your brain off. If you paid attention to your thoughts, you would quickly discover that most of them were useless and unimportant. This inundation of non-stop, toxic thinking can cause people to feel anxious, overloaded, and overwhelmed. This is the realm of intrusive thoughts.

Intrusive Thoughts

Unwanted and intrusive thoughts are thoughts that are stuck in our heads. It is like hearing the lyrics of a song over and over again, and you can't make them stop. These thoughts may revolve around work, our decisions, or our relationships.

We can have intrusive thoughts on any topic, especially if a powerful emotional charge is tied to it. Worry and rumination are the most common forms of persistent negative thinking, but we cannot leave out the voice of our inner critic as we explore intrusive thoughts.

Rumination

Rumination is when we obsess over an upsetting situation. We are ruminating when we relive the details of an argument with a friend repetitively in our minds. People often ruminate when something frustrating, threatening, or insulting happens.

Rumination starts out simple enough. There is a sincere desire to solve a problem or make sense of a situation. A solution to the issue is fleeting. Individuals who ruminate are often afraid to take the steps needed to confront a situation. Their lack of outward action causes them to keep returning to the perceived offence in their mind in hopes of a different outcome.

Worry

Worrying is similar to rumination. The critical difference between the two is that ruminating people focus their mental energy on resolving past events, while worriers concentrate on the future. Worry is a cycle of living with the question 'what if' in the forefront.

When we worry, we imagine a tragic potential outcome to an unknown event. We worry in an attempt to solve suspected problems in our lives. We all have moments when we worry. When our thoughts become persistent and uncontrollable, this is when they can become a cause for concern.

Worry can be the first stage in a much larger negative thinking process. It often underscores the manifestation of its more insidious forms: anxiety and panic, with worry on the mild side of the spectrum and a full-blown panic attack on the other.

Our Inner Critic: The Voice Of The Ego

Then there is our inner critic. Our inner critic is intricately connected to our ego, which exists on subconscious levels. It is the voice inside our head that tells us we are too fat, too stupid, too slow, or too lazy. It might also remind us that we are not good, deserving, or important enough. Often it is relentless and cruel. It acts as judge, jury, and executioner. It has no qualm in maliciously pointing out all of our flaws and foibles.

Think about the hurtful commentary flowing through your mind. Does it consume a great deal of your attention? Does it speak to you like an angry parent? Our inner critic reveals to the conscious mind all of the destructive thoughts, ideas, and opinions we have about ourselves and others. This voice can be brutal. Who needs someone else to beat us up or erode our self-confidence when we will gladly do it to ourselves?

The Subconscious Mind

Our incomplete understanding of the mind leaves us believing we consciously control our lives. We think we are the masters of our ships and can choose our destiny, but our subconscious mind secretly runs the show. The subconscious mind sits below our ordinary waking consciousness. It manages the vast majority of our lives without us even knowing it. It works in the background and behind the scenes. It is where much of our thinking originates, including everything we have yet to be aware of.

We take in and amass so many things in our subconscious mind. It is a veritable storehouse of information. It stockpiles what were once conscious thoughts and records them for later use. It is filled with the experiences, ideas, impressions, perceptions, memories, opinions, and judgments we acquire throughout our lifetime. We might not be aware of its presence, but it influences us nonetheless.

You can think of the subconscious mind as a giant computer hard drive that records the entirety of the impressions you receive and files them away for safekeeping. It stores every experience and every encounter you have day in and day out. Part of its job is to interpret and organize our world. It looks at similarities between new encounters and compares them with our past experiences. From this analysis of old versus new, a conscious thought is formed.

Some of this data exists just below the surface in our preconscious mind. This layer acts as a bridge between our conscious and subconscious. Information stored in the preconscious can include thoughts, ideas, and memories that can be readily brought into our conscious awareness.

It only requires an act of recollection or an association with a previous experience to draw it into our conscious experience. It can be likened to a search engine. When we type in what we are looking for, it digs through all of the data stored in the subconscious mind and brings it to the forefront for us to pick and choose from.

The Nature Of The Subconscious Mind

As children, we arrive in this world with a clean slate. We are filled with joy, spontaneity, creativity, playfulness, and love. We are free of constraints and experience the world with an innocent sense of curiosity and wonder. As the days pass, our parents, siblings, elders, peers, and life events slowly influence us.

Our younger brother looks up to us with admiration, leaving us feeling important. We feel successful when we win the spelling bee or bat in the winning run at the baseball game. Similarly, when a favorite toy is mistakenly thrown away, a wished-for red bicycle is not received at Christmas, or a close friend moves away, we can feel hurt or sad.

The emotions we experience during these situations can have a profound impact on us. If felt often enough and consistently enough, they can manifest as a core belief. These beliefs set the stage for how we see ourselves and how our lives should be.

Core Beliefs

We all have positive thoughts that make us happy, optimistic, and productive. We also have negative thoughts, which can cause us to feel anxious, depressed, or guilty. If these thoughts are repeated often enough, they can become habit-forming.

Over time we stop questioning their validity. We accept them as an accurate representation of ourselves and our world. This creates the foundation of our personal belief system.

Our core beliefs can leave us seeing ourselves as bold, confident, and courageous. We might lead an army uphill into battle in search of victory. On the other hand, we might perceive ourselves as a frightened, incompetent failure where we drop our shoulders in defeat and say, *"Why bother?"*

Our success or failure, movement or lack of movement, action or inaction all depends on our personal perspective. It can spur us on or throttle back the full expression of who we are.

We all carry positive and negative core beliefs about ourselves. We might feel strong, self-assured, or bold in certain instances, while we might feel like a failure, worthless, unlovable, invisible, broken, or ugly in others. Pick your poison. And, in case you were wondering, yes, we all have more than one core belief that controls how we express ourselves and interact with others.

We Are Borg

Perhaps a more straightforward way of looking at our core beliefs is to view them as little computer programs. Our active programs are habitual patterns we use when responding to a situation. These fixed strategy scripts are usually a playback of a previously held conscious thought. They work by subtly directing how we feel and act.

Our scripts sit in the background, waiting for us to turn them on. Once stimulated, they operate the same way every time. Like our neural pathways, the more we respond to life happenings in a particular manner, the more dominant the program becomes.

We don't need to be aware of our thoughts for these internalized programs to exert their influence over us. All that needs to happen is for something to 'trigger' one of them in order for it to take over. Triggers can cause us to react to a seemingly minor stressor that bounces off one of our core beliefs. The slightest reminder of a harrowing event, a color, a smell, a sound, or even a feeling can set off a person with an associated trigger. A war veteran who hears a car backfire and automatically ducks for cover is a classic example.

Our lack of knowledge of our inner world causes us to give our subconscious mind too much control. Many times, we are unaware a program has been activated or why. This can cause us to become a servant to our programming without realizing it. We can end up reenacting old, outdated, harmful patterns over and over again.

Scripts take away our ability to think and act on our own behalf. They cause us to become disconnected from our true inner nature, our true wants, needs, and desires. It is only by bringing these patterns into our conscious awareness that we can ever change, fix or eliminate them and return to the innate person we came into this world being.

The Ego Strikes Back

Something even more calculating lurks in the darkness of our subconscious mind, and that is the ego. Our recurring thoughts, opinions, life experiences, and core beliefs form the ego's foundation. It is the image we have of ourselves which we project out into the world. It tells us who we are, *"I am strong, smart, dashing, and desirable,"* even if that truth is based upon other people's opinions of us.

We are all a bit egotistical. The ego is overly preoccupied with our survival, the accumulation of material wealth, and our success. It has an intense need to feel superior. Let's be honest with one another. A small part of us always wants to see ourselves above everyone else. We want the big house, the fancy car, whatever will help us to rise above other mere mortals. When we are experiencing this compulsion, it is our ego talking.

Our ego also likes to tell us what to do and how to do it. It will remind us how much harder we should be trying, providing us with a long list of things to accomplish. *"If I do these things, I will finally fit in, be appreciated, or be seen."* Once completed, the ego is never satisfied. It never savors a job well done. It is always hustling for more. This can leave us feeling anxious if we are not working on our next goal, achievement, relationship, or the object of its desire.

Sometimes it is hard to recognize when the ego is running the show. It tries to trick us into identifying with it. It says "*trust me.*" It wants us to believe that its opinions are facts and the truth of any given circumstance. It will offer insights and advice, but its guidance is not coming from our inner wisdom but through the lens of our past experiences and core beliefs. It blinds us from knowing who we really are, from understanding the person we were born to be by ensuring we reject anything that falls outside its preprogrammed beliefs.

Sitting behind the mask of the ego lies all of our insecurities. Another one of its functions is to protect the tender parts of ourselves from emotional harm. Challenges to the ego manifest in several ways. It may attempt to make an impression on others through its status, be that knowledge, possessions, or good looks. The ego may try to get attention by creating a scene, telling everyone about its problems or illnesses, or offering others its unwanted or unsolicited opinion. Complaining, self-justification, clever arguments, distorted facts, and one-upmanship are standard tools it will use. It might bubble up to the surface through our inner critic, where it uses its spiteful voice to criticize or belittle us or others.

Some people live their lives through the lens of the ego. Egotistical people consistently think about themselves. They are self-absorbed and invested in the 'I.' *"I want." "I feel." "I need."* They want to feel bigger, stronger, and faster than everyone around them, especially since they know more, have more, and perceive more than you. You are inferior or inadequate in their masterful eyes.

Egotistical people constantly judge their self-worth based on those around them. Moreover, they do not like to see themselves in a 'less than' position. When they feel diminished, they will strike out in an attempt to repair their fragile egos.

Their security is often boosted when they assert themselves using anger and aggression. This leaves them feeling more in control. They might react to a perceived slight by becoming annoyed. The aggressive outbursts they display make it easier for them to manipulate you and get you to alter your behaviors in their favor or on their terms. Their fight-type strategy covers up the powerlessness and pain they feel inside. A person with their ego engaged will not listen to or respect you because they, at least in their mind, are right while everyone else is wrong.

In truth, our ego is our enemy.

My ego always pushed me to do bigger and better things. To say I was a workaholic is an understatement. If I did 'this,' I would at last be noticed. I could become rich and famous like the Looney Tunes character Elmer J. Fudd who would introduce himself as *"I am Elmer J. Fudd, millionaire. I own a mansion and a yacht."* His repeated expression was my milestone in life. To only own a mansion and a yacht.

My ego told me to return to school, write another book, and publish more articles. It directed me to host a podcast and develop a training program. It didn't stop there. My ego gave me specific instructions to follow. Most of the projects it assigned had tight deadlines. There was always something to do and never enough time to get it done.

And then, when I finished one project, it would immediately be time to start another. It never allowed me to savor my successes, pat myself on the back or dwell on my accomplishments. Instead of feeling satisfied, I only experience a vague sense of relief. The perpetual internal pressure to go, go, go – do, do, do was over. I could breathe, at least for a little while. I had always thought these imperatives were divinely inspired. Now I can conclusively see the truth. It was my ego in sheep's clothing.

The Stories We Tell Ourselves

The ego maintains its stronghold over us when it fills in the missing and, in many cases, erroneous details about a person, place, or situation. We have been telling stories, our myths, and legends of old, long before pen was put to paper and stylus was put to clay. We find tales of epic battles, torrid romances, elaborate and intricate plots, scandals, and conspiracies. Some follow the hero on a heroic journey, while others take us on flights of fantasy. These stories often contain a nugget of truth, which was elaborated on over time.

The same holds true of the stories we tell ourselves and others. It can be a happy tale, one that boosts our worth, or it can be one filled with pain, upset, fear or hurt. One need only think of the fisherman who catches a 3-pound bass, but to the rest of the world, it was a raging behemoth that took every bit of his strength to reel it in. Granted, a fish was caught, but the truth of the event was distorted to transform a humdrum event into a glorious tale.

Anecdotes, like this fish story, are an apparent ego-boosting white lie we might perpetrate on others. The narrator of this yarn knows they were fibbing, sharing inaccurate details of their adventure, but this is not always the case.

We often believe the stories we tell ourselves, complete with the unsound, imaginary details we use to fill in the blanks. The stories might range from how we are God's gift to humanity to the other end of the spectrum where our world is going to come to a complete and disastrous end. The accounts we conjure up depend on our core beliefs, which sets the stage for the unfolding tale.

I'm sure any parent can relate to this narrative. Your 16-year-old child, Mattie, goes out with her girlfriend Dani for the evening. She is expected home by 10 pm. The appointed hour comes, and she has yet to return. This is where the story begins, and the account running through Mattie's mother's mind takes on a life of its own.

> "It's 10:15, and Mattie isn't home yet. I haven't heard the car pull up or the door open. What's going on? Is she ok? Who did she go with? Oh yea, she went with Dani. Dani is unreliable. Didn't she recently get in trouble at school? That Dani is a troublemaker. I never liked her.
>
> Maybe they met up with some boys. I hope not. God forbid she gets pregnant. Then what will happen? Will she have to drop out of school or skip college? I will be so disappointed with her if this is the case.
>
> Oh, but what if they got into an accident? Maybe they are hurt. They could be stuck in a ditch off the side of the road. I will give them 10 more minutes to get back before I call the police."

Like the tales of old, this story started with a nugget of truth. Mattie missed her 10 pm curfew. Mattie's mom, now triggered, endeavors to understand what is happening. Based on her core beliefs, her ego jumps in and automatically begins filling in the details and coming to conclusions without having all of the facts.

We tell ourselves stories all of the time. When they take on a life of their own, they can become challenging to deal with. We have all had situations where something happens, and our mind goes wild.

As the story gets bigger, we naturally become more anxious. Our heads may start spinning out of our control. We may begin to worry or ruminate, with each new imagined detail only amplifying the situation, until we find ourselves deeply ensconced in negative thought. Once in the midst of a story, especially a fun, meaty, or juicy one, it can be hard to stop its forward momentum.

So, what really happened to Mattie? Mattie did not enter the house at the appointed time. This was a fact, the nugget of truth in this tale. Mattie and Dani were sitting in Dani's car out front. She was not out on some wild adventure, she wasn't in the hospital, and she wasn't with a boy. They arrived at Mattie's house at 9:30 pm, got into a riveting conversation, and Mattie lost track of time. On the other hand, Mattie's mom worked herself up into a frenzy by envisioning a series of falsehoods in her mind.

Once you become aware of the concept of stories, it becomes easy to see them in others. You may notice this well-honed skill in some of your friends or family members. Heck, you might even be able to catch yourself spinning one of these yarns.

Final Thoughts

Unconstructive thinking and negative core beliefs are not the only things taking up space in our conscious and subconscious minds. We can also have positive ones. Would you believe it is possible to shift the dynamic of what is happening inside, tossing toxic, harmful thoughts to the wayside and bring better ones into your reality? Stay tuned! We will explore how to do this later on. Our next stop is another aspect of our being that exists in our inner world: our emotions. They play an integral role in how we act and react to the world around us.

Me And My Emotions

"Embrace your emotions. They are there to teach you about yourself. Suppressing your emotions is suppressing yourself."
- vendulap.com

Our thoughts, emotions, and behaviors are all interconnected, but the process always starts with a thought. They underscore everything. According to the American Psychological Association (APA), an emotion is *"a complex reaction pattern involving experiential, behavioral, and physiological elements."* Particular thoughts inspire the way we feel, encouraging distinct emotions. How we feel can lead to specific behavioral responses. While we can control our thoughts and we can control our behaviors, we can't control our emotions.

Our emotions, nevertheless, are not just things that happen to us. Emotions serve a real purpose. Our emotions are the moderators between our thoughts and actions and are pass-through experiences. They are how our bodies react to a perceived situation and are outside our conscious control. This rapid and autonomous bodily response system provides us with first-hand, instantaneous information about our thoughts.

Our emotions help us navigate our environment safely. They offer invaluable insights into what is important to us, which we can use to guide our decisions. They let us know how we feel about a particular item. Do we like it, or do we find it distasteful? These subconscious judgments allow us to make positive and lifesaving choices before all of the data is in. Whether we realize it or not, our emotions profoundly influence our daily lives.

What would we do without them? How would we be able to determine what we want to do at any given moment? We would not experience the joy of going for a walk on a warm summer day or the thrill of opening gifts on Christmas morning. Nor would we be able to walk away from a toxic relationship because of the suffering we have endured. There would be no excitement, there would be no satisfaction, and there wouldn't be any pain. The decisions we make, the activities we choose, and how we respond to an encounter are all based on our emotions.

The word 'emotion' is often interchanged with the term 'feeling,' but feelings are not emotions. An emotion is a more complex kind of feeling and is experienced on a deeper physiological level. Feelings derive from conscious sensations and perceptions we have about our bodies. They are subjective experiences. We feel pain or pleasure, comfort or discomfort, hunger, thirst, hot or cold. We can contemplate and question our feelings. On the other hand, emotions are not a conscious reflection of our internal environment but an uncontrollable reaction of the subconscious mind.

Our emotions are constantly in flux. They transition from one to another throughout the day. They come and go. Not a moment goes by when we are not feeling something. We assume we are in touch with our emotions, yet by default, we typically don't pay much attention to them until a strong, usually negative one, arises and erupts in our lives. We often just find ourselves feeling a certain way and do not understand what we are sensing or how we got there in the first place.

The activation of our emotions happens like this. Something happens, and we have a thought about it. The thought bounces off our internalized beliefs and life experiences and activates an emotional response within us. It only takes 100 milliseconds for our bodies to react emotionally to a thought and another 600 milliseconds for our brains to register the emotional reaction. This means it takes less than a second for a thought to elicit an emotion and for our body to provide feedback of this reaction to the brain. Okay, this is slower than the speed of light, but it still is really fast.

Our emotions set into motion a series of physiological changes based on the scripts we have labored on over the years. How we react depends on how we interpret a situation. Sometimes our thoughts will activate an intense emotional response, and at other times, not so much. It doesn't matter if our perception of an event is misconstrued, inaccurate, incomplete, or just plain wrong. Our subconscious mind responds so quickly we often don't realize we have reached an internal conclusion.

Some of the determinations we make are nurturing, while others are destructive. They will either serve us or set us back. Each time we reenact a script, we reinforce the emotional response and the habitual patterns we are already familiar with. Even if we decide to not take any action, which might be an active program in our inner world, we are making a choice notwithstanding.

Think about a time when someone said something unkind. It may have been easy for you to keep your composure and take it in stride. You might get angry, burst into tears, or shut down emotionally at other times. Perhaps in the first instance, you readily recognized the person speaking was a dolt, while on the second occasion, the person sharing their hurtful view was someone you love or respect. They may have used the same words, but you had a completely different reaction.

Emotions And Emotional Regulation

Having and experiencing emotions is a normal part of our lives. Everyone has them. When we effectively manage our response to an emotional situation, we demonstrate good emotional regulation. Emotional regulation is the ability to handle how we feel by controlling our emotional state, including how we experience our emotions and express our feelings. Having healthy emotional regulation allows us to cope, bounce back from and stay calm during challenging circumstances.

Imagine something frustrating happens to you, and you get upset. Internally there is an upsurge of emotions brewing inside. You might want to scream, yell, throw something, or curl up in a ball and cry. People who display healthy emotional regulation will often take a few deep breaths or count to ten before taking action. It buys them time before they act or react to what was triggered. This slight pause can curtail a sudden impulsive, emotional response. It gives them the time to restore rational thinking and objectivity to what has just transpired.

Everyone's emotions spin out of control every once in a while. For some people, their feelings can seem overwhelming, like a wild roller coaster ride. Their inner world gets so caught up in a destructive cycle of intrusive thoughts is hard for them to stop. This can cause them to respond to an event in an over-the-top way, where they can find themselves lost in their emotions and become emotionally dysregulated.

People who have issues with emotional regulation trigger quickly. They are more emotionally responsive and are often challenged with the ability to control the overwhelm they feel inside. They experience intense emotions more frequently, on a grander scale, for a longer duration and feel like they have no control over them.

These individuals may feel anger or rage. They may display aggressive behaviors or 'freak out.' They may blame or accuse others or lash out before they know all the facts. They may break down in tears or overreact to what seems like a non-issue. Internally they may be experiencing fear, guilt, sadness, frustration, self-loathing, worthlessness, or abandonment. This all happens many times before they can stop themselves.

In addition to the whirlwind of emotions they are feeling, people who suffer from emotional dysregulation frequently do not know how to stop the onslaught of feelings they are experiencing or how to reduce their intensity. Upsetting situations tend to quickly bring up strongly felt emotions, making it difficult for them to recover. Emotionally dysregulated individuals have a hard time letting go of irrational thoughts and quieting their minds. Once activated, they cannot stop thinking about a situation even when, on a rational level, they recognize it is time to move on.

Issues with emotional regulation aren't a death sentence when talking about changing our inner nature. If you find that you have a tendency to emotionally dysregulate, help is on the way.

Fight, Flight, Freeze, Fawn

Negative emotions, in particular, tend to trigger more intense responses, best seen in the classic fight, flight, freeze, or fawn response. Our stress response system instinctively activates when we perceive a threat, real or imagined, causing us to take on a defensive posture. We all use a combination of these stress responses. Which one we use depends upon which active program gets triggered.

Within milliseconds, our amygdala, an almond-shaped structure in the brain, activates a sequence of well-orchestrated and near-instantaneous physiological changes. Its activation is designed to protect us from life-threatening physical, mental, and emotional challenges. Its goal is to minimize or avoid danger.

Sometimes, we react emotionally to a set of non-critical perceptions where our life is not at risk. We have all had this happen. You are at home, safe and sound, eating popcorn and watching a scary movie on TV. As the eerie music rises, your anticipation grows. You find yourself getting nervous. Your body tenses up. Your heart begins beating faster. Then something unexpected occurs, and you jump. Even though you know there is nothing to be afraid of on a conscious level, except maybe your own imagination, your mind-body connection responds to what it sees on the screen.

Our stress response system operates in three ways. We will try to fight back, attempt to run away (flight), or freeze in place. In recent years, a fourth stress response has been added: fawn. You might see yourself and how you traditionally react when adversity strikes as we go through each category. One response type might traditionally take the lead and act as your default reaction, but we all engage in each of these survival patterns at different times.

The Fight Stress Response

We engage our fight response when we instinctively believe we can overpower a threat. Individuals employing this response type will attack the source of danger. Our fight response is extremely valuable. It ensures we have good boundaries, healthy assertiveness, and will protect ourselves when required.

For fight types, their fight response may become their primary way of addressing any and all dangers. Fight types believe they have to preserve their life at all costs. They believe they can create safety for themselves through power and control. These individuals, when threatened, utilize anger and rage to intimidate or shame others into submission. Many individuals who display narcissistic tendencies are trapped in the fight response.

Fight types often feel a deeply ingrained sense of intense anger, have explosive outbursts, or display aggressive behavior toward others. They walk around feeling agitated or confrontational in all of their encounters. They might find themselves grinding their teeth or walking around with a tight jaw. They may want to punch someone or something when upset or will stomp around, slam doors, or kick things. They may glare at people, give them the evil eye, raise their voice, or talk to them in a mean or hostile tone.

The Flight Stress Response

We can tell we are engaging our flight response when we retreat from a disagreement, especially when we realize fighting will only make things worse or the opposing force is too powerful to overcome. The physiological changes our bodies experience, instead of preparing us to fight with our fists blazing, we use it to escape. Ultimately, the flight response helps us to disengage from an altercation by retreating.

Children, for example, will run away from something that scares them. We may do the same thing as an adult, but its form often becomes subtler. We are in flight mode when we are confronted by someone, and instead of arguing, we turn around and walk away. Folding our arms during an uncomfortable situation can also indicate the flight response in action.

People who gravitate toward the flight response may find that they are constantly busy. Workaholic is often a word tied to individuals who are flight types. They may find they are always rushing around, have a hard time sitting still, or feeling relaxed. If they are not doing something, they are planning or worrying about what they will do next. In excess, flight types may have obsessive thinking, worry excessively, or experience chronic anxiety or panic.

The Biology Of The Fight Or Flight Stress Response

The activation of the sympathetic nervous system is tied to our fight-or-flight response. We draw upon the sympathetic nervous system to mobilize us into a protective stance.

When activated, the sympathetic nervous system releases the neurotransmitters adrenaline and noradrenaline into the body. These hormones help prepare us for the physical demands of doing battle with the enemy or running away from the scene.

The mobilization of our sympathetic nervous system causes our heart to race and our blood pressure to increase. Our muscles tense, our veins constrict, and our pupils dilate. Our blood sugar may shoot up while our digestive and immune systems shut down. We may begin to breathe deeper, sweat, feel shaky, anxious, or panicky during these stress-filled moments.

If fighting or running fails to ensure our safety, we naturally go to 'plan B,' where we engage our parasympathetic nervous system. It assumes control if our subconscious mind believes there is no way to fight our way out or escape a harrowing situation.

The Freeze Stress Response

The freeze stress response is like the fight-or-flight response on hold. When engaged, we become paralyzed in fear. Imagine coming up on a deer walking through a field. Instead of running away, the deer stops dead in its tracks and stares. It is trapped in the freeze response.

When we employ the freeze response, our subconscious mind quickly realizes there is no way we can defend ourselves. We cannot defeat the dangerous opponent in front of us nor run away from it safely. Freezing becomes our next best option. The goal of freezing is to stop the predator from spotting us in the first place. We try to make ourselves invisible and disappear.

The freeze response is often seen in children, especially those who experience a large amount of trauma. They are too small to fight with their parents. They could not run away either. This can leave the child feeling powerless and unable to protect him or herself, and their only choice is to freeze up, numb out or dissociate.

The freeze response can play out in different parts of our lives as an adult. Freezing can leave us feeling mentally or physically paralyzed. There may have been a time when you went to a job interview, had to speak in front of a room full of people, or were sitting down for a final exam. With eyes wide open, you found your mind going blank. You were freezing.

The freeze response might cause us to have a hard time making meaningful decisions for ourselves or acting on a decision once made. Vocalizing our truth or being honest with ourselves may also be challenging. Freezers often clam up when around new people who seem threatening. Freeze types often find comfort in the safety solitude offers. Freeze types often suffer from something called 'dissociation.'

Dissociation: A Freeze Response Byproduct

We all dissociate at one time or another. Many times, we are not aware of it when it is happening. What does it feel like? We are dissociated when we lose touch with our immediate surroundings. When we are daydreaming, we are dissociating. We are dissociated when we drive our cars to a location and don't remember how we got there. When we get lost in a movie or a book, we are dissociating.

We are also dissociated when we 'space out' while a friend is talking our ear off or our boss is yelling at us, and we let it go in one ear and out the other. In relationships, we often hear of situations where one partner will 'tune out' the other partner's complaints. Dissociation.

When threatened and realizing we cannot escape from a dangerous situation, freeze types will disconnect from what is going on by emotionally distancing themselves. Dissociation helps them deal with what might otherwise be too emotionally devastating to bear.

We no longer feel the enormity of what is happening, which might be intense fear or helpless when we are dissociated. Dissociation allows us to block off our thoughts, feelings, and, ultimately, our memories of a frightening encounter. Our consciousness shuts down to minimize the intensity of the disturbance.

When someone is dissociating, they may experience their body go limp or rigid. Time may slow down. They may have mastered the art of changing their internal channel whenever an incident becomes uncomfortable. Some may experience complete separation, where they may feel like they are looking down at themselves from outside their own body. From this perch of safety, they can observe events unfolding around them as if they are watching a movie or are in a dream.

Some individuals may vividly remember each threatening incident but view it from a detached, unemotional position. Others may not remember what happened at all. This can include the circumstance or their feelings about the event. They may even have gaps in their memory. This does not mean that they did not suffer its ill effects. They have just buried the memory of the situation deep within their subconscious mind.

The Biology Of The Freeze Response

The body, when the freeze response is triggered, instead of releasing adrenaline to power our fight or flight stress system, releases opioids to protect us from physical and/or emotional pain. Opioids are the brain's natural pain relievers and can be likened to taking morphine or heroin. This causes the heart rate to slow down.

Thinking can become incredibly difficult as blood is diverted from the brain. We might hold our breath, have difficulty getting words out, or feel our throats constrict. We might also feel cold, shut down, or numb to what is happening. Our eyes may look fixed, and we may appear spaced out. We might find ourselves fatigued, dizzy, or depressed. Our body posture may collapse, or we may want to curl up in a ball and hide.

The Fawn Response

The last stress response we may employ as protective armor is the fawn response. According to psychotherapist and author Pete Walker, people who have unsuccessfully tried to respond to challenges by fighting, running away (flight), or freezing may find, by default, they have begun to fawn.

Fawning refers to the flattery or affection one may display to gain favor or advantage. Fawning is the opposite of the fight response. Instead of aggressively attempting to escape from a dangerous situation, fawn types attempt to avoid or minimize confrontation. They do this through what is referred to as 'people pleasing,' where they bend over backward, trying to be nice. It is not done because they are being considerate to the other individual but employ it to protect themselves.

Unlike our other stress responses, the fawn response is not built into us. It is developed and honed into a defense mechanism in early childhood. The fawn response often begins to emerge before the self develops, many times even before we start to speak. The toddler who finds him or herself trapped with a caregiver who expects to be pleased and prioritized quickly learns to submit to the abuser's will. They discover being obedient and helpful is the only way to survive parental maltreatment. They realize protesting, objecting, or engaging their fight or flight response in opposition to the caregiver's wishes will only elicit even more frightening parental retaliation.

This causes the child to surrender their own will and put their personal feelings aside to feel safe. They ascertain that their needs are less important than their desire to steer clear of more abuse. They recognize there is a modicum of safety in being compliant. The cost? They forfeit their rights and preferences or be broken – a submissive slave. The child learns to omit the word *"No"* from their vocabulary. This interferes with their ability to develop a healthy sense of self or assertiveness.

Fawn types often lose all sense of self by the time they are an adult. They fear the threat of punishment each time they want to exert themselves. Regardless of the situation, interrelations with others can feel like a war zone, where the individual waits for the next blow to come. Any hint of danger triggers servile behaviors where they willingly give up their rights and themselves.

This response pattern of taking care of others is so deeply ingrained into their psyches that they often do not realize they have given up so much. They find safety when they merge with the wishes and demands of others. Fawning serves as the foundation for the development of codependency.

Emotional Addiction

I know, I know. The section heading sounds really bad, but it is something we need to discuss and put squarely on the table. We all have times when we are in a bad mood. It is normal and part of being human. Some of us, however, experience negative states deeper and more frequently than others. This brings up the concept of emotional addiction.

Neuroscientist and pharmacologist Candice Pert, in her appearance in the movie *The Secret*, asks viewers, "What emotion are you addicted to?" I never forgot that line even though years have passed since I saw the film. I could easily name a few contenders for my own emotional addiction, but emotional addiction is not a topic that is often discussed in the literature.

Addictions are often thought of when referring to drugs, alcohol, gambling, work, or sex, but we can also become addicted to our emotions. Living constantly in a perpetual state of fear, anger, sadness, frustration, or worry can have a devastating impact on our bodies. These persistent toxic states always underlie chronic disease and stress-related disorders. They can be just as destructive to our well-being as drinking and drugging.

When we have an emotional addiction, we become hooked on feeling a certain way, a familiar way. If much of our childhood was lived in fear, then we might be addicted to the feelings frightening situations hold. We can become addicted to worry or the adrenaline rush that stress offers. We can become preoccupied with a person or situation and the ensuing feelings our obsession offers. Even though the emotions we are experiencing might not feel good to us, in actuality, they might be excruciatingly painful, there is still a strange part of us that finds comfort in them.

Many times we will attract people or situations into our lives that will give us more of what we are asking for. If we need to feel minimized, ashamed, talked down to, or humiliated, we might find an abuser who will activate these feelings within us. This will allow us to feed our cravings. The more we give into an addiction, the more time we give it, ponder it, hold it in our awareness, or savor it, the more entrenched it becomes. Like any true addiction, we can build up a tolerance to the emotions we are feeling and need to go to an even deeper, darker place within ourselves for longer expanses of time to get our fill.

Sometimes our emotions can become so strong they can seem like they have taken control of our lives. In his book *A New Earth*, Eckhart Tolle discusses a phenomenon he calls the 'pain body.' He contends the pain body feeds off of our negative thoughts and their associated emotional responses. Just like the alcoholic, who needs one more drink and then another to feel good, he believes you can start to crave negative emotions the bigger your pain body becomes.

People with emotional addictions can look for the most insignificant events to trigger an emotional response to nourish their yearning. This allows them to experience a rush of negative emotions, a distorted kind of emotional high. These individuals typically thrive on things being slightly out of balance. Their lives may be filled with constant drama where they go from one crisis to another. Anything less leaves them feeling numb. The world would be a boring place without this ongoing rush.

You might have an emotional addiction if you are always sad, complain about everything, or only see the negative side of a situation. You might have an emotional addiction if you repeatedly tell the same tragic story. Ironically, many of us thrive on our negative emotions. They may be the only ones we know. We can become so accustomed to this toxic state, even if it leaves us feeling uncomfortable, that it seems normal. In fact, to many, the negative feelings seem so familiar they are like the old comfortable pair of slippers we put on at night. They can leave us feeling weirdly safe and at home with ourselves.

Sometimes we try to divert our attention from painful emotions by turning to drugs or alcohol. We might find things to focus our awareness on. This includes working, watching television, or spending time on the computer. Some people turn to gambling, sex, or spending money to help them cope with what they are working to avoid. The more we indulge in these behaviors, the less pain and discomfort we feel.

Thankfully, our emotional addiction isn't always front and center. Typically it will rear its ugly head when we react to a particular trigger. The slightest bit of activation can bring it out of the shadows, where it can take over our thoughts and behaviors. It will remain active until we can calm our inner world and return to our normal waking self. Sometimes, we can go on emotional benders that can last for days or even weeks. I have come to recognize that when I am triggered and end up in my rabbit hole, I am actively feeding my addiction.

My Potluck From Hell

One year, the company I worked for was planning a Christmas potluck celebration. I worked with my husband, and we decided to bring in a joint dish as our contribution. I was going to make my extra super meaty baked beans. Excited about my menu selection, I purchased many of the ingredients: a giant can of beans and a pound each of bacon, ham, and ground sausage to put into my masterful concoction. This easily set me back $15.00.

The date of the potluck was fast approaching. The woman coordinating the affair asked me what I was bringing. I informed her, my husband, and I would supply a large pan of extra meaty baked beans. Exasperated, she flatly stated each of us, my husband and I, had to bring separate dishes. *"We weren't allowed to combine our efforts."* She wouldn't budge from her position even after I detailed my recent purchases.

I was pissed, especially considering some highly paid coworkers committed to bringing a couple of liters of soda or some store-bought rolls as their contribution. Well, this sent me into a tailspin. I immediately found myself within the bowels of my own negative thinking. I got to visit my rabbit hole.

My ego and inner critic were working on overdrive as I ruminated about what had happened. I can only imagine what I was like. 'Bitch' is a great word to use if I were to describe my attitude. It wasn't the first time I had found myself dissociated and living within the dark chasm of my mind.

I remember this story so clearly, not because I can recall any of the horrid things that went through my mind or anything that occurred while I was in my rabbit hole, but because of what happened next. Someone made a wisecrack or told a stupid joke. I don't know.

Regardless of what they said, it made me laugh. It was as if the clouds parted. I could see sunshine peaking through the storm clouds that surrounded me. I could breathe again. It felt like whatever I was holding on to was finally melting away and draining from my body. I remember thinking, *"I'm back!"*

In hindsight, I have come to realize that what happened in my inner world had nothing to do with the potluck, baked beans, or having to bring something else (which I was never going to do because I am hard-headed and, at the time, really bitchy). It had everything to do with my internalized fear of verbal confrontation. My inability to tell the coordinator what she could do with her unfair rules set me off. It took me almost two weeks to return to the surface and find myself again. Not fun, but I guess my emotional addiction got a good feeding!

Tolle also suggests, *"People with strong pain bodies often reach a point where they feel their life is becoming unbearable, where they can't take any more pain. Inner peace then becomes their priority and their lives have the chance to turn around."* I can only imagine how big my pain body was. Ginormous would be my guess.

As Echart suggested, my life did become unbearable. I couldn't take it anymore and all I wanted was inner peace and the chance to feel happy. One of the unsung beauties of pain is that it forces us in a new direction. I guess I really needed to experience a lot of pain to at long last exit stage left.

It's All About The Chemistry

Not to make excuses for our behaviors but… We each have our own unique set of thoughts, emotions, and emotional responses. Our programming and past experiences set the stage for how our bodies and minds will react. When we experience a particular emotion, our body releases a flurry of powerful chemicals known as neuropeptides into the body.

Each emotion is associated with a specific neuropeptide. These small chains of amino acids enter the bloodstream and activate or inhibit the function of our cells. Peptides regulate every aspect of our body, including the production of chemicals such as adrenalin, dopamine, cortisol, and serotonin, which can affect our mood. They operate as a lock and key mechanism of cellular expression.

Each cell is covered with a series of 'receptor sites' that act as the locking mechanism of the cell. When a specific neuropeptide (the key) comes into contact with a cell, it can bind to a receptor. Thus, when the key (the peptide) is inserted into the lock (the receptor site), it can lock or unlock it, turning cellular function on or off, depending on the peptide.

Sorry for that complex cellular biology explanation, but this is where it gets compelling. If we have a propensity to experience a particular emotion, our body automatically recalibrates itself to accommodate it. As our cells divide and new ones are created, the new cell has increased receptors on it to handle the predominant neuropeptides our bodies are producing. We literally transform our body to be able to deal with more negative, unhealthy peptides just by consistently feeling angry, anxious, worried, frustrated, or ill at ease.

The increased number of receptor sites cause us to feel a specific emotion quicker and more intensely because we can process them faster. It is like when the grocery store opens up an additional checkout lane, and we can quickly move through the process instead of standing in line and waiting.

Interestingly, as negative emotion receptor sites increase, the number of receptor sites that support feel-good chemicals like dopamine, serotonin, and endorphins decreases. This was a shocker to me. We are teaching our bodies to be more inclined to negative thinking with each troubling thought we have. Equally as interesting, as we change our thoughts to happier and healthier ones, the number of harmful receptor sites will diminish, and the ones associated with feeling good will increase. With time and practice, we can literally transform ourselves into a whole new person from the inside out.

Emotional Addiction And Abuse

Before we move on, I would like to discuss a sensitive topic that often confounds our rational minds. It has to do with abusive relationships. Many wonder why individuals stay in abusive relationships. Part of the reason is their body chemistry. We are wired to connect with others. Part of that connection comes in the form of two neurotransmitters, oxytocin, and dopamine, both of which play a crucial role in why someone willingly stays in a toxic situation.

Oxytocin is known as the 'love hormone.' It is released when we hug, kiss, cuddle, or connect with someone we love. It causes us to become naturally attached, as in the bonding of a parent to a child or with our romantic partner. Dopamine leads to feelings of pleasure. It is our body's reward system. It gives us that 'high' feeling when we do something we enjoy. It also motivates us to go back and get more.

There is a profound intensity when a relationship with an abusive partner begins to unfold. Called 'love bombing,' they will inundate you with attention, phone calls, and texts. They act like they want to spend all of their free time with you. You are their one and only, the apple of their eye. They often appear as your knight in shining armor or your soul mate.

It feels good to be with them. You find yourself enjoying each and every minute you spend together. They come off as being overly interested and eager to develop an intimate relationship quickly, which causes your oxytocin and dopamine levels to soar. Their behavior can be very confusing to even the best of us.

The hidden goal of people with abusive personalities is to get you hooked on them. Over time things begin to change in the attitude of the toxic person. Their true selves slowly emerge, and so do the challenges, especially when they detect you have become comfortable or complacent in the relationship.

It is not unusual for an abuser to withdraw their affection or become mentally, emotionally, or physically abusive. Their actions often elicit the fear of being hurt or abandoned by them, causing your cortisol, your stress hormone, to spike. You feel awful inside as if your world is coming to an end. This can leave you with an intense desire to repair the relationship, especially if you have old unhealed wounds. There is an involuntary and often overwhelming need to recreate the intensity and connection you had grown accustomed to. You want to experience the hormonal high again.

Then reconciliation occurs. They become attentive again, apologize for their transgression and swear it will never, ever happen again. Your body floods with dopamine, the reward hormone, and you feel good again. The cloud has lifted. More oxytocin is released as your connection is re-established. You begin to feel safe once more.

This cat-and-mouse game is repeated over and over again, increasing your dependence on oxytocin and dopamine. It does not take much time before you will do whatever is required to avoid another incident and the giant chemical fluctuations you feel inside. It is said that it is easier to go through heroin withdrawal than recover from the chemical dependency of a 'trauma bond.' This makes it is also easy to see why some people stay in intolerable relationships and find it nearly impossible to leave. It's their chemistry.

Final Thoughts

Attunement to our emotions offers us many gifts. We can use them to better understand ourselves. They are a great tool to use as we pilot our way through life challenges, where they can help us make decisions that benefit our overall happiness level. Our emotions are also wonderful at indicating when there is a problem, telling us *"something isn't right."* People who are emotionally aware tend to have better relationships, improved self-esteem, and lower anxiety levels.

Today, however, our thought processes and emotional reaction are often so neglected, most people are oblivious to the deep currents that move through them, hold them back, and lead them astray. The involuntary nature of these inner-world processes leads us to conclude we have no control over them and are powerless to change them. The good news, and a considerable focus of where we will be venturing next, is learning how to navigate and modify these experiences.

The Self-Awareness Game

> *"There are many ways to calm a negative energy without suppressing or fighting it. You recognize it, you smile to it, you invite something nicer to come up and replace it; you read some inspiring words, you listen to a piece of beautiful music, you go somewhere in nature, or you do some walking meditation."*
>
> - Thich Nhat Hanh

There is no shortage of unhappy, depressed, anxious, fearful, obsessive, hostile, and violent people in the world. Mental health practitioners have increasingly relied on incorporating drugs such as antidepressants, mood stabilizers, or antipsychotics to fix the discord we experience in our inner world. They assume we suffer from some kind of pathology or a brain chemistry imbalance these marvels of modern medicine can miraculously cure.

A happy person's brain does differ from an unhappy person's. Our brain chemistry also does not cause our unhappiness. Our past has a great deal to do with how we feel today. Our life experiences, our thoughts, beliefs, ideas, emotions, emotional reactions, and the internalized scripts we have created are what set the stage for how we feel inside.

It's easy to get caught up in the predictable patterns of our existence. Our conditioned habits cause us to become oblivious to what is happening around us. We go through our daily routines like an automaton, never altering from the tried and true. The first step in taking charge and seizing control of our lives is to turn off our autopilot and start living consciously.

Author Samantha Case identifies conscious living as *"a lifestyle that is driven by an intention to navigate your life with a malleable sense of self-awareness that fuels your choices and directly impacts your experience of life and your interactions with the world."* Living consciously is about bringing awareness into every aspect of our being. It is about actively deciding rather than blindly accepting whatever falls in our path. It is about taking ownership of our lives, and living the life we want, on our own terms. The more conscious we are, the more power we have to shape our reality.

Living consciously prompts us to question our internal programs and challenge the status quo. We can use it to emancipate ourselves from the control our ego has exhorted over us for years. It is liberating. We can use it to begin breaking down the detrimental neural superhighways we have created and open the door for developing new ones. It can free us from the ongoing cycle of negative thoughts, explosive emotional reactions, and harmful behaviors that have caused us a lifetime of pain and suffering. The act of conscious living can transform us and our everyday existence.

Self-Awareness

Many of us do not understand how we tick. If we don't know ourselves, it is difficult, if not impossible, to identify what we are thinking, how we are feeling, or why we are acting a certain way. Turning inward is a game changer, with self-awareness at the core of renovating our inner world. It is the single most powerful practice we can employ to shift from unhappiness to ecstasy.

According to psychologists Shelley Duval and Robert Wicklund, self-awareness is *"the ability to focus on yourself and how your actions, thoughts, or emotions do or don't align with your internal standards. If you're highly self-aware, you can objectively evaluate yourself, manage your emotions, align your behavior with your values, and understand correctly how others perceive you."* How would you know what to change if you are not aware there is a problem in the first place? By paying attention to our internal qualities, we can make bigger, better, and bolder choices about our lives and ourselves.

When we know what we are thinking and feeling, we can decide what to say or do next. It offers us additional choices, more possibilities, and potential outcomes. When our awareness is lacking, we can be easily influenced by outside sources instead of our inner truth. Unawareness takes away our power to decide for ourselves. It is the epitome of living on autopilot.

Self-awareness can improve every area of our life. As we peel back the layers of our ego, we may discover new things about ourselves, our strengths and weaknesses, our old wounds, and the emotional poisons that create vulnerable, reactive places inside. We may discern new ways of looking at what is going on or uncover a novel strategy to help us rewrite an old script or preprogrammed response.

Self-aware individuals recognize their internal standards and act based on these values. This allows them to identify clear boundaries and stick to them instead of spiraling into an emotion-driven response to uncomfortable circumstances. This increased awareness enables them to take responsibility for their thoughts, emotions, and actions. Anything less, they are not being genuine, honest, or authentic to themselves.

William Walker Atkinson, in his 1908 classic *The Inner Consciousness*, offers this analogy. *"Compare the mind to a bowl of muddy water, into which a clear stream of fresh water was pouring. Anyone will see that the fresh water will gradually clear the entire body of water, until the muddy substances are not discernible."* He continues and tells us, *"If you wish to drive away the darkness, just open the shutters and admit the light."* Awareness is the fresh water and the light that will drive away our inner darkness.

Mindfulness

Becoming increasingly aware goes hand in hand with another inward-looking concept called 'mindfulness.' Mindfulness refers to the act or the process of being present in the moment. In his book *Interbeing: Fourteen Guidelines for Engaged Buddhism*, Buddhist monk Thich Nhat Hahn says, *"Only the present moment is real and available to us. The peace we desire is not in some distant future, but it is something we can realize in the present moment."* We are not distracted by rehashing our past or worrying about our future when we are in the 'Now.' Our past is but a memory, and our future has yet to unfold. All there is and will only ever be is the here and now.

Being in the present moment naturally offers us a respite from the non-stop chatter in our heads. It slows down our thinking. We can more readily see the truth of circumstances occurring around us from this place of calm peace. Life unfolds before us without preconceived notions. This allows us to make wiser, more conscious choices instead of permitting our thoughts and emotions to rule. It turns off our autopilot and lets us become the decider of our own fate, the captain of our ship.

Our ego is often running the show when we are operating on autopilot. It lives in our thoughts of the past and future, the incessant conversations in our heads, and the fantastic stories we tell ourselves.

Moving our awareness into the present moment, even for a brief moment, turns our ego off. It deactivates our onboard computer and disables the preprogrammed scripts of the subconscious mind. There is no place for the ego when we tune into ourselves. It has no choice but to fade into the background.

Typically, we focus our attention on anything that comes our way. *"Oh, look, a squirrel!"* We can quickly become lost in our thoughts if we do not pay attention to them. The small step of noticing what we are thinking or how we are feeling is the nature of mindfulness. This small act naturally returns us to the present moment.

It is a clear indicator that you are not in the present moment when you find yourself trapped in a cycle of worry or rumination or if you are having a heated debate with your inner critic. You are not in the 'Now' if you are thinking about a person or situation. When you are restless, anxious, or unable to relax, you are also not in the present moment.

A research study by the University of Wisconsin discovered that even a short-termed practice of raising our awareness through mindfulness vastly improves our ability to calm down and emotionally regulate. Additional studies have shown individuals who take up mindfulness practices experience less stress and increased mental performance over those who do not.

Here is the difference between self-awareness and mindfulness. Self-awareness is about exploring and understanding all that goes on inside. Mindfulness helps us to calm down and connect with ourselves and our surroundings in a deeper, more meaningful way. It naturally slows the chaotic flow of thought that run through our brains which can lead to uncontrollable emotional ups and downs. Combined, these two practices give us the ability to examine ourselves and begin to identify the underlying thoughts or core beliefs that are setting us off in the first place.

Said another way, mindfulness provides us the space we need to inwardly examine ourselves. It shuts off the ego. We are no longer lost in our thoughts, ruminating about the past, or worrying about the future. It increases self-awareness, allowing us to get to know who we are as individuals. Together they can assist in identifying our bad habits, our outdated triggers, and the unwanted behaviors that maintain power over us. It is no surprise one would go hand in hand with the other.

New Mantra For Living

Awareness begins and ends with the decision to tune into what is happening inside. Think of it as a journey, a life-long journey that constantly evolves as we learn and grow. Granted, it is easier to live our lives on autopilot but becoming more mindfully aware of our inner world is astonishingly simple to do. It does, however, require motivation, willpower, and self-discipline to achieve lasting results. This inner wisdom supports us as we take steps to change what hurts us, limits us, or keeps us in self-destructive patterns.

Transforming our inner world necessitates us to be honest with ourselves. It is not about becoming perfect but about accepting the good and bad aspects of our being that may come into our awareness. We also have to be willing to step outside of the comfort zone our autopilot provides and be amenable to trying something new. Given a bit of time, attention, and focus, you will be amazed at the results you can achieve.

I am hoping by now you are willing to trust me just a smidge. I am going to ask you to make a small leap of faith. No, we haven't gotten into the meat of how we will bring about these vast, huge, life-altering changes, but the price you have already paid for your suffering has been far too great. If you have read thus far into this book, it must seem clear that what you are doing isn't working, so it may be time to try something different. Maybe it is time to commit to yourself just like you would commit to a romantic partner. Take a deep breath and say with me, *"Nothing is more important to me than feeling good."* See, that wasn't so hard.

So are you ready? Then let the games begin!

Your Inner World Awaits

You can do hundreds of things to bring you back into the present moment. In fact, any activity that focuses the mind can be used to lead you to the best version of yourself. Traditional methods call for the incorporation of meditation, guided imagery, or yoga. These are not the only ones. You can employ a vast array of other techniques to help you tune into what is going on inside. All of these approaches will support you to organically achieve a calm, relaxed state.

Don't worry, we will get into a slew of them as we move forward, but by way of introduction, I want to present something straightforward to start. We will begin our practice of focusing the mind on an activity we are all familiar with: breathing. Deep breathing is one of the simplest mindfulness practices you can use to bring you back into the present moment, increase your awareness, and help restore a sense of inner peace.

We have all had moments when we have felt stressed. Maybe you experience it when you were getting ready to walk into a job interview, a big test, a meeting with your boss, a sit down with your partner, or a situation with an uncertain outcome. You may have found yourself taking a nice deep breath to help calm your nerves and regain your composure. This unconscious yet voluntary act played a significant role in your ability to quiet the anxiety you may have been feeling inside.

Let's give it a try!

Take a deep breath. That's right, a nice deep breath and then let it out. Take a moment to notice how you are feeling. Perhaps you didn't sense any change at all, and that's fine. On the other hand, you might have detected you were feeling a bit lighter, a bit more relaxed, clearer, or more present. All of this occurred because you took a single breath.

Breathing is something we do all day and night without even realizing it. We take more than eight million breaths per year. That's about 666,666 a month, 22,222 a day, 925 an hour, and 15 per minute. Breathing is essential for life. We can only survive a few minutes without taking a breath.

Our breathing is a largely automatic, involuntary process controlled by the brainstem, the same part of the brain that regulates our heartbeat. Unlike our heart, we can consciously control our breathing whenever we like. It is the only bodily function we have voluntarily and involuntarily control over. Mindful breathing is the conscious act of taking slow, rhythmic, deep breaths.

"Breath-focused meditation can be an entry point of bringing you to a mindful place, accepting the present moment for what it is. Your breath is the one true thing that is present in the moment — you can't breathe ahead, and you can't breathe backwards," says Megan Elizabeth Riehl, PsyD, the Clinical Director of the GI Behavioral Health Program at the University of Michigan. The Mayo Clinic suggests, *"There's sufficient evidence that intentional deep breathing can actually calm and regulate the autonomic nervous system."*

There is intentionality to deep breathing. Jon Kabat-Zinn, author of the internationally acclaimed book *Wherever You Go, There*

You Are, had this to say. *"The breath is the current of life, connecting body and mind... it helps to have a focus for your attention, an anchor line to tether you to the present moment and to guide you back when the mind wanders, the breath serves this purpose."*

Mindful breathing is a powerful and highly recommended tool you can use to help you find your way back to the present moment. It forms the foundation of every meditation and mindfulness practice. There is no overt objective to mindful breathing other than paying attention to your breath.

Andrew Weil, M.D. informs us that *"Practicing a regular, mindful breathing exercise can be calming and energizing and can even help with stress-related health problems ranging from panic attacks to digestive disorders."* Conscious breathing is beneficial when something unsettling happens or when you are aware of internal tension or stress. If you are worrying or ruminating about something, breathe!

The Science Of Breathing

You may be wondering why breathing is so powerful. Deep breathing affects the chemical and physiological activities in our bodies. It also activates the vagus nerve. The vagus nerve, runs from the brain to the abdomen. It oversees an array of bodily functions, including mood, heart rate, and our breathing. It represents a primary component of the parasympathetic nervous system. Activation of the parasympathetic nervous system turns off or down-regulates our fight or flight response. It helps slow everything down and restores a sense of calmness and relaxation in the body.

Deep breathing is the fastest way to stimulate our vagus nerve and activate our innate relaxation response. This is why we usually feel better after taking a few deep breaths. It reduces our stress to a manageable level automatically.

It tells the amygdala, the brain's fear center, that we no longer need to be at 'code red.' Activating our parasympathetic nervous system lets the body know we are safe. The regular use of deep breathing is beneficial if we routinely default to fight or flight mode when upset or discover our sympathetic nervous system is chronically active.

Working With The Breath

There are countless ways you can practice mindful breathing. Which one you choose is totally up to you. Traditional breathing practices recommend sitting comfortably or lying down with your eyes closed. Then concentrate on bringing a deep, slow breath in through your nose into your abdomen and lungs and exhaling it slowly out of your mouth. Focusing your attention on your breath will let your chaotic thoughts melt away. Mindful breathing really is this easy!

Breath Counting

One very simple breathing method is called 'breath counting.' All you need to do is close your eyes and breath. Let your breathing be natural, ideally slow, deep, and rhythmic. Count each breath on the exhale until you reach the count of five, and then start your count over again. Breath counting looks something like this:

Breathe in, breathe out – one

Breathe in, breathe out – two

Breathe in, breathe out – three

Breathe in, breathe out – four

Breathe in, breathe out – five

You will know your mind has wandered if you count up to seven or eight. Don't worry about it if you do. Just start back at a count of one and keep breathing. Do two to three rounds of breath counting as part of your daily practice.

Box Breathing

Box breathing is another powerful yet effortless breath technique. Its goal is to help return your breathing to its normal rhythm. It is advantageous to use after a stressful experience. You can perform box breathing until your inner calm returns. Box breathing involves four basic steps, each lasting to a count of four.

Breathe in through your nose - to the count of four

Hold your breath - to the count of four

Breathe out through your mouth - to the count of four

Hold your breath - to the count of four

If you find holding your breath to the count of four taxing, you can try counting to three instead. If you want, you can extend your cycle and count to five or six. The important thing here is that each leg of the box is the same length. Try incorporating four to ten box breaths per session as part of your daily practice.

The 4-7-8 Breath Exercise

The 4-7-8 breathing exercise is similar to box breathing and equally straightforward. There are only 3 steps to this method.

Inhale through your nose - to the count of four

Hold your breath - to the count of seven

Exhale through your mouth - to the count of eight

Ideally, try to do at least four 4-7-8 breaths when you start with this exercise. You can extend this practice to eight breaths as you feel more comfortable. Also, try slowing down your breathing as you become more proficient with the technique. This will help you achieve a more profound sense of relaxation.

Color Breathing

Some people enjoy working with colors as they deep breathe. You can draw in one color, such as the friendly, warm feeling inhaling the color yellow might offer or the fiery passion red breathing may stimulate. When you exhale, you can pick a different color. Many practitioners like to imagine exhaling a dull brown or grey tint to represent the mental and emotional toxins they are discharging. There isn't any set method tied to color breathing. It can easily be incorporated into whatever breathing technique you desire. Below is a list of colors and their associated emotions.

Colors And Emotions

Color	Emotion
Red	Passionate, aggressive, warmth, comfort
Orange	Playful, energetic, stimulating, exciting, joyful,
Yellow	Happy, friendly, warning, optimism
Green	Stable, growth, harmony, tranquility, creativity
Blue	Serene, trustworthy, inviting, calmness
Purple	Luxurious, mysterious, romantic, wisdom
Pink	Feminine, love, calming, gentle, romance
Brown	Earthy, sturdy, stabile, comfort, organic
Black	Powerful, sophisticated, edgy
White	Clean, virtuous, healthy

Breathing On The Go

Did you try any of the breathing exercises above? If you did, what did you think? How did it feel to be a silent witness to what was going on inside? What was it like to pay attention to how long and deep you inhaled, the sensations of your lungs as they inflated with air, and then the release of your breath as it exited your mouth? Did your world calm down? Perhaps you felt clearer, more focused, or more present after you tried. Maybe you were able to take a step back and could differentiate you, the thinker, from your thoughts.

You can practice mindful breathing throughout the day. A few minutes here and a few minutes there can offer life-changing results. With just a tiny amount of effort, deep breathing can become an unconscious part of your daily life. It all starts with making the conscious decision to focus on your breath each day. Some people work with their breathing first thing in the morning and just before bed in the evening, but don't let this limit the number of times you bring your awareness to your breath and experience the power of being in the present moment.

Now that you have breathing basics under your belt, you can take it on the road. You can select any place or activity and use it as another occasion to practice breathing. What activities do you engage in regularly? Use your imagination. Pick a time and location that best suits your lifestyle. Make it something doable for you. Better to do a little every day consistently than to do a lot for two or three days and then forget about it altogether. Try to get into the habit of consciously breathing while you are:

Breathing On The Go Locations

Stopped at a red traffic light

Waiting for the microwave to chime

Sitting at work

Breathing On The Go Locations
Continued

Washing dishes

In the restroom

In line at the supermarket

At the doctor's office

Walking the dog

Lying in bed

Trying Mindfulness On For Size

Breathing isn't the only way to move your awareness into the present moment, but breathing is a great place to start, especially if you are new to the whole self-awareness game. You can become mindful of all you do anytime! Eating dinner or washing dishes, walking, talking with friends, brushing your teeth, or exercising your body are all excellent opportunities to turn your focus inward. All you need to do is slow down and pay attention. Spending time alone with your television, computer, or phone off also supports a mindful practice. It creates a space where you can reflect and detach yourself from others and the day's activities.

Still feeling unsure of this whole mindfulness thing? Hopefully, this example will give you a better idea of what I am discussing.

Let's say you want to be mindful while taking a shower. Pay attention to turning on the water faucet. Take in how it feels to step into the shower and under the streaming water. Sense the warm water as it flows over your body. Notice each body part as you lather with soap and rinse it off. Enjoy the peaceful feeling of being one with yourself as you move through this process. You never know. You may never look at taking a shower in the same way again.

Mindful Eating

If you have ever read a weight loss book, one common suggestion is to slow your eating to give your body time to register what you have consumed. What the authors didn't share, as you worked to battle the bulge, is they are teaching you how to be mindful. You do not have to have weight issues to practice mindful eating. You can use it as a meditative tool to bring you into the present moment. Who knows. You might drop a few pounds while you are at it.

It all starts with eating slower, but there are some nuances to it that will support the mindfulness aspect of this practice. Some suggest eating at a table and serving your food on a plate. All too often, we eat a sizable amount of food standing in front of the refrigerator or munching delectable tidbits right out of the bag. Turn off the television, and put your phone away. Eliminate other distractions if possible. Then you are ready to begin.

Take your first bite and put your utensil down. Savor the flavor. How does it taste? What does the texture feel like in your mouth? Try to masticate each mouthful 10 - 25 times. When you are done chewing; swallow. Perhaps take a few breaths before taking your next mouthful,

This, like breathing, sounds so simple, so basic, but many of us have the habit of scarfing down our meals in five minutes or less. Think about how mindful you will be as you focus on each bite before taking another. Give it a try. Mindful eating might be more challenging than you think.

Mindful Tapping

Another excellent mindfulness exercise you can try to help restore balance to your body is called 'tapping.' Tapping is derived from the ancient Chinese medicine healing tradition of acupuncture. Precepts tied to acupuncture state a series of 12 channels, 'meridians,' travel through our body similar to our blood vessels. These vessels correspond to our internal organs and are associated with specific emotional states. Discordant feelings clog up these channels, similar to the plaque we might have in our arteries.

During acupuncture treatments, small needles are inserted into specific meridian points to activate and clear these buildups. Tapping, like acupuncture, stimulates the meridians and dislodges accumulations. When these vessels are clear, we feel happy, calm, and unfettered by negative emotions. Tapping is like getting an acupuncture treatment without the needles.

Tapping calms the nervous system and interrupts our fight-or-flight response. The simple act of activating specific meridian points sends calming signals to the amygdala, which stimulates our parasympathetic nervous system. This helps quiet our central nervous system, release stress and negative emotions while imbuing our bodies with feelings of peace.

There are 12 major meridians that run through the body. Tapping focuses on 9 of the 12 meridians.

Tapping Point Locations

No.	Location	Associated Organ
1	Side of hand	Small intestine
2	Top of head	Governing Vessel
3	Eyebrow	Bladder
4	Side of eye	Gallbladder
5	Under eye	Stomach
6	Under nose	Governing Vessel
7	Chin	Central vessel
8	Collarbone	Kidney
9	Under arm	Spleen

Start at point #1, in the figure, side of the hand. Often referred to as the 'karate chop point,' tap this location. I like to tap to the count of 7, but you can select any number of taps you want. Move on to the next point when you are done activating the karate chop location, and continue from one point to another.

Deep breathing is highly recommended as you tap each point. Slow down your tapping if you find yourself racing to the end. This will increase the sense of relaxation you will experience.

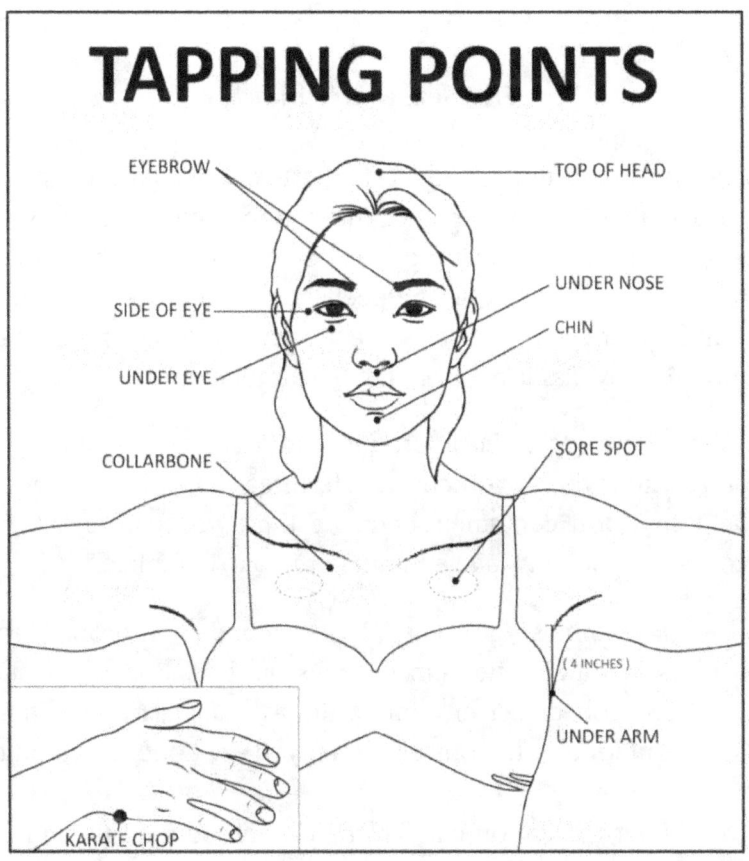

You can do one round of tapping; you can do two, three, or five. In fact, you can tap for an entire hour. How long or how often you do it is entirely up to you. Practice tapping throughout your day when you are feeling good and when you are feeling down. In addition to the benefits of activating our meridians, this method gives us something to do, something more tangible than breathwork alone. It offers an activity, like doing yard work or cleaning our house, without ever having to get up off the sofa.

Five Senses Grounding

Like most mindfulness practices, the five-sense grounding can be done anywhere or anytime. This method helps you shift your focus from what makes you anxious to what is happening around you. This exercise is especially helpful for people whose traditional stress response is the freeze response, where they automatically dissociate from the here and now.

Here's how to do it. Look around and identify five things you can see, four things you can touch, three things you can hear, two things you can smell, and one thing you can taste. This exercise should only take a minute or two to complete.

- Five things you see: Take a good look around and select a specific item to focus on. How does it appear? Do you detect any interesting details? List these items out loud or to yourself. When you are done, move on to the next.
- Four things you can touch: Reach out and touch four things or take a moment to feel the things you are wearing, such as your shirt, your shoes, etc. How do they feel to you?. Are they hot, cold, rough, or smooth to the touch? What else do you notice about these items?
- Three things you can hear: Listen to what is going on around you. Are birds singing, cars driving by in the

distance, or children playing? Can you hear the air conditioner or refrigerator humming?
- Two things you can smell: Take a deep breath and take in the smell of your surroundings. Was the grass freshly mowed? Is there something cooking in the oven? You can also take a whiff of your clothes, your skin, or even the objects you just touched.
- One thing you can taste: Take a bite of something or a quick drink. What does it taste like? In a pinch, you can practice this on yourself. Can you detect the flavor of the last thing you ate?

There isn't any rhyme or reason to the things you see, touch, hear, smell, or taste. It is all about focusing your mind and awareness. This will return you to a state of calmness in the present moment.

Asking Questions

Becoming mindful of the happening of your inner world sets the stage for digging a little deeper into what is going on inside. One way to begin tuning into your thoughts, ideas, feelings, and motivations regarding a situation is by asking and internalizing questions. In short, self-reflection questions encourage us to venture into the uncharted waters of our subconscious mind. They empower us to look at our own stuff.

Reflection questions can help us to see things in a different light or for what they really are. They can aid us in identifying our unhealthy preprogrammed scripts or the wild stories we might be telling ourselves. Hopefully, with new insights, we can make different choices that will bring us different results.

This investigation into ourselves has a positive secondary effect. It will automatically bring you back into the present moment, all while you learn more about yourself. It helps establish the practice of inner exploration, which is an invaluable tool when an obstacle or challenging situation comes to the forefront. It also provides you with hands-on experience opening yourself up to receiving answers from your superconscious mind, a topic we will explore later.

Many people who work with self-awareness questions will typically document their findings by 'journaling.' Journaling, in and of itself, is a mindfulness practice. It gives us something to focus on. It naturally calms down our stress response system and can help untangle the crazy going on inside. Putting pen to paper makes it easier to detach from the situation at hand. This opens the door to accessing the more elusive parts of our psyche where we can bypass our ego and draw forth our true thoughts and emotions.

A journal is no more than a notebook that captures our impressions in one place. Plenty of fancy journals are available on the market, but you can use a spiral notebook just as well. By having all of your writing together, you can go back and review what you were thinking at a specific moment or evaluate the progress you are making. Some people journal every day as part of their mindfulness practice. Others utilize this tool when problems arise. How, when, and where you journal is up totally to you. Suffice it to say the information that may come up from the depths of your being can be awe-inspiring.

Self-reflection questions can cover any aspect of your life. Below is a small array of topics you can use as a starting point. But don't stop there. Try asking questions about different aspects of your life. What do you love, and what kinds of things do you hate. Dig into your habits, your preferences, the kind of work you want to do, or the type of relationships you want to experience. There are no right or wrong questions, only revelations. If you feel stuck and cannot think of something meaningful to explore, hundreds of websites offer inner awareness writing prompts.

Questions

What really matters to me?

What accomplishments am I most proud of?

What areas of my life need work?

What things do I love about myself?

What things do I want to change about myself?

What makes me happy?

What triggers anxiety, fear, or sadness in me?

What kind of future do I want for myself?

What is something I want to do but am too scared to try?

Working Through Issue

Here is another set of questions for you to try. These writing prompts can be used when you are triggered and feel angry, upset, anxious, overwhelmed, or annoyed and want to understand why. They can also be employed when you would like to identify your role in a past event that may still have a hold over you. Pausing and identify our thoughts, feelings, and behaviors, shines a light on a situation. It helps us discover important information about ourselves.

You can use the questions below to focus on a current experience or a past one. They can help to you unravel circumstances where you found yourself upset or explore situations that ended with a less-than-desirable outcome. They can help reveal your reasoning, rationale, fears, ingrained beliefs, and deeper motives. Understanding why you acted or reacted in a certain way or reached a particular conclusion gives you the power to change.

Questions

What hurt the most in this situation?

Which of my needs were not being met?

What was I thinking in this situation?

What emotions am I feeling?

What stories did I tell myself?

What pattern am I detecting in this situation?

What is the worst thing that can happen if I take 'X' action?

What small changes can I make to have a better tomorrow?

When I am hurting, what is the kindest thing I can do for myself?

If I had one piece of advice to give myself, what would it be?

What did I learn from this situation?

The Battle Over Chinese Food

I would have never figured it out if I hadn't taken the time to reflect on what was going on inside. It wasn't long ago that I was heading back from a conference. It was dinnertime, and I was hungry. I could have gone home and found something to eat, but I didn't want to cook. I was in the mood for Chinese food, yet as I tried to wrap my mind around stopping at the restaurant, a cascade of negative thoughts entered my mind.

My inner critic promptly reminded me I had plenty of food in the refrigerator. It went on and on about how I would save money by eating there. I was befuddled. I had worked all day and was ready to relax, so why was I fighting with myself. This wasn't the first time I've battled my inner critic over spending money. This was, nonetheless, the first time I took the initiative to question myself to understand why. Being thrifty was what initially came to my mind. There was no big revelation on that front. As I pursued other lines of inquiry, what I uncovered was more than I had bargained for.

I discovered spending money was not the end of the equation. It was the trigger. Digging through the layers of my mind, I uncovered an ancient program. The program said, *"No!"* My inward look brought up the realization that I had stopped asking for anything I wanted at a young age. I knew the answer. It would be *"No, negative, nada."* What emerged was a realization of how I had been denying myself the things I wanted for years.

My inner questioning uncovered this habit and helped me recognize the presence of an active script that was implanted long ago. With this knowledge in hand, I can now be more mindful when this trigger gets activated and take steps to love myself a bit more. Cross your fingers for me on this one!

Final Thoughts

This may be hard to believe, but we cannot force our brains to change by desiring it. Long-lasting transformation also does not happen overnight because we made a single decision. It takes time to create a foundation of growth, nurture new habits, internalize fresh and updated scripts, and reconstruct the neural pathways of our mind, but it is worth the commitment and effort. Change is achieved thought by thought, situation by situation.

So remember, practice, practice, practice, especially when the world is good, and you don't need it. Try it on for size, discover a method that works best for you, and experience first-hand its relaxing effect. Then when you find yourself in the middle of a negative thought, a stress-filled situation, are anxious, fearful, or overwhelmed, you will already know what to do. In time you may readily turn to one of these methods rather than rush to activate one of your old preprogrammed scripts.

The Courage To Change

"It takes bravery to break old habits, to turn to the voice inside your head and say, "I will not let you speak to me that way." It takes courage to sit down and have a conversation with your mistakes. Growth is uncomfortable; it's slow and rarely steady, but I promise you that nothing in full bloom will ever tell you that the struggle wasn't worth it."

- srwpoetry

Becoming mindful and raising our awareness to what is going on inside is critical when talking about transforming our lives. Yet, there is another piece to the puzzle that needs to be addressed and acted upon. This is the preprogrammed scripts that, in essence, have been running our lives. We all do things automatically, whether it's moving through our day-to-day activities or the impulsive reaction we have to an uncomfortable predicament.

Do you wake up in the morning and immediately go to the kitchen to get a cup of coffee? This rote series of steps is an unconscious ritual many of us follow. Like getting a cup of coffee, many of our preprogrammed scripts are harmless. But what about all of the unconscious programs we consistently reenact that bring pain and suffering into our lives? It would behoove us to begin raising our awareness to these pesky patterns to see what falls out. Once a harmful script is identified, we can use it to change our inherent programming for good.

Perhaps one day, after a fight with your partner, you begin to evaluate your relationship. Your curiosity causes you to start questioning yourself, your motives, your behaviors, and more. You might realize you have a knee-jerk reaction whenever they behave a certain way. Suddenly the light bulb goes off, and you plainly see the negative pattern, the preprogrammed script that is contributing to your relationships woes.

Now, I am not talking about their behavior, but the automatic response inside you. This awareness may cause you to question why you are thinking, feeling, or acting in a certain way. You might uncover the fact you consistently run away from embarrassing situations, attract toxic people into your life or erupt when something doesn't go your way. But why? And this is the whole point, to discover why.

We cannot change what we are unaware of. Many times these scripts were installed when we were very young or in a vulnerable position. We often assume this is who I am, but it is not. It is the 'real you' with one of your computer programs running. Some people have likened these harmful scripts to a computer virus. When you feel overwhelmed, trapped in a cycle of negative thinking, or are hanging out in your rabbit hole, you have just encountered one of your own personal blue screens of death. Nothing works right. The problem isn't you! It's the virus. This insight, this bit of increased awareness will make it possible for you to delete the harmful program or rewrite the script.

One good way of discerning active scripts is to look for patterns in your thoughts, feelings, and behaviors and watch how they play out in real-time. You may become cognizant of the underlying dynamics of one of your behaviors. Maybe it has come to your attention some of your thoughts are setting off a cascade of uncontrollable emotional responses. In fact, you may come to realize that some of the scripted patterns you reenact are toxic, maladaptive, and destructive to your well-being.

With practice, you can gain the skills needed to begin recognizing what specific thoughts are activated, which emotions are triggered, or what behavior is creating trouble. You can use this information to devise a modification plan. This identification will create the opportunity to intervene when a thought needs to be redirected, an emotional response is running out of control, or when a behavior is making matters worse. The more specific you can be in identifying the most troubling issues in your life, you can use this information to introduce changes into these problematic areas.

If you suspect your negative thoughts are activating troubling emotions and behaviors, examining them would be a good idea. If your actions seem to be the culprit, then focusing on your behaviors would be more appropriate. By breaking down these component parts, you will gain clarity on where and how to intervene when trouble arises. Hopefully, these insights will also help you begin managing your inner world more successfully.

It doesn't matter if you decide to focus on your thoughts first. So be it if you want to address your actions or begin by paying attention to your emotional responses. You are developing a mindfulness practice, one specifically designed for you. Start with the one that seems the most obvious, most pressing, has been on your mind the longest, or seems easiest to access. This is your practice, so whatever you begin with is perfect! With the entry point you choose, you can start unwinding your inner world until you reach the chewy surprise inside - an ongoing sense of peace, calmness, and happiness.

Identifying Our Stuff

We often think we are basically positive, optimistic people. Granted, we all have our moments, but if the study by the National Science Foundation is correct and 80% of our waking consciousness is trapped in cycles of negative thinking, then I don't feel alone in my emotional turmoil.

This extraordinarily high number leaves me to believe we all find some eccentric pleasure in our pain. Who would have ever thought so many of us regularly feel bad inside? But it is what it is, and the data speaks for itself. We're all messed up!

For some reason, people tend to pay more attention to the bad things that happen to them versus the good. We get a flat tire driving to work. Instead of accepting the situation, our ego jumps in to save the day. It might weave stories about how the universe has a vendetta against us. It might arouse our *"I can't get a break"* core belief where we willingly get on our pity potty and wonder, *"Why me?"*

No one wants to get a flat tire, but the reality is, the things that happen to us are neutral, neither positive nor negative. According to experts, all the unhappiness we experience exists in our minds. The root cause? Our obsessive, negative, ego-driven thinking.

It is not the event itself but our attitude towards it. Our reactive, toxic thoughts and emotional responses are the most traveled roads for many of us. They keep us trapped in a perceived hostile, vengeful world regardless of what good is happening around us. It is no wonder why so many of us are depressed or anxiety filled.

Society generally is not interested in exploring the brighter side of our nature. It silently suggests we should always feel positive, living in an ongoing state of perpetual bliss, or else something is wrong with us. At the same time, we are never taught how to be content with our lives, let alone ourselves. Our lack of understanding causes us to get caught up in the ego's mind games, where we focus on what we don't have or how our lives should somehow be different.

The ego's automatic programming causes us to put off feeling happy until some expectation is achieved. We won't be satisfied until we have more money, lose weight, finish a project, get married, or have children. We are led to believe that happiness is just around the corner or maybe the next.

Like a mouse on a wheel, we end up striving for what we don't and may never have, desiring something that will always be just out of reach. We will never be able to grasp the golden ring when we are caught up in the ego's rat race. How can we ever feel satisfied or content if we can't stop chasing the fairy tale of how our lives should be? This programming seems keen on keeping us broken and unhappy. Maybe you've never thought of this before, but this belief, this *"I need to have this or achieve that before I can be happy,"* is yet another preprogrammed script.

We all have the power to change our old, outdated, harmful scripts. We have already started this process by raising our awareness to the activities of our inner world. We can use this awareness to make better choices about the type of thoughts we allow into our conscious minds. Benefits of this deliberate control dramatically change our emotional reactions and likely behaviors. It also has the effect of modifying our emotional set point, our body chemistry, and our relationship with the world around us.

Again, where you choose to begin the change process is totally up to you. For our purposes, we will start by raising our awareness to our emotions and emotional state. We will move on to modifying our thoughts and behaviors from there.

Emotional Awareness

Unlike our thoughts and behaviors, our emotions are not under our conscious control. They are the byproduct of our thought process. We can, nevertheless, use them to gauge what is going on inside. It is a clear indicator we are having unconstructive thoughts when uncomfortable or distasteful emotions arise. We can take advantage of the sensations we are feeling and use them as a preverbal roadmap to our inner world.

People who are unaware of their emotions are often controlled by them. They may believe they are powerless to change them, causing them to live in a state of constant strife. Life can be frustrating, annoying, or perplexing because they are unsure of or numb to what they are sensing at any given moment. We all tend to mire around in our own funky emotional place, but we rarely use the discomfort we are feeling as a chance to tune into its message. We often assume the feeling 'is' the problem and not a symptom of something more profound.

Being in touch with our emotions helps us to handle them more appropriately, particularly when we become cognizant of the ever-changing array of feelings we experience throughout the day. It all starts by tuning into this vast landscape without judging it. We have spent so much time ignoring our emotions they might seem like a stranger from a strange land, but there is hope! We can learn to discern them and bring them into conscious view.

Noticing And Naming our Emotions

A clue to how you are feeling is revealed in your physical sensations, how your body feels when particular emotions are stimulated. Having to say something unpleasant may leave you with a lump in your throat, while a tight feeling in your chest might indicate apprehension. These physiological symptoms are a direct reflection of your current emotions. Other signs of uncomfortable, painful, or even toxic emotions can include constantly feeling overwhelmed or irritable, having trouble relaxing, feeling stressed out, or withdrawing from activities you once enjoyed.

We can further identify what is going on in our internal environment by labeling our emotions. The ability to put our feelings into words is a potent tool. By developing an emotional vocabulary, we can categorize our feelings more effectively.

The classification and identification of emotions have been debated for centuries. Some claim we have over 250 distinct emotions, while others identify five primary emotions, then secondary and tertiary ones. Regardless of the official count, many of us can only consciously recognize a small handful, such as happy, sad, angry, or mad. We might not be able to comprehend when we are angry until we erupt in a full-blown rage, much less be able to differentiate between feeling angry when what we are really experiencing is frustration.

Labeling our emotions allows us to reflect on our feelings and enables us to uncover their cause and potential impact on our life. Focusing on our emotional state is also a mindful practice that will calm us down. To help you get started, below is an extensive list of emotions. You can use it as a reference guide to get a better handle and a more precise identification of what you are actually experiencing.

List Of Common Emotions

Acceptance	Aching	Adoration
Affection	Aggressive	Agony
Alienated	Alone	Amazed
Amusement	Anger	Animosity
Annoyed	Anxious	Apathetic
Apologetic	Appreciative	Aware
Awe	Awkward	Baffled
Bitter	Bitter	Boredom
Calm	Carefree	Cautious
Challenged	Cheated	Cheerful
Cold	Comfortable	Compassion
Confident	Confused	Contentment
Courageous	Cowardly	Cranky
Craving	Craving	Cruel
Curious	Curious	Defeated
Defensive	Delirious	Denial
Depressed	Desire	Desperate
Destructive	Determined	Disappointed
Disapproval	Disgust	Disgust
Dislike	Dismay	Distracted
Distress	Doubtful	Eager

List Of Common Emotions Continued

Embarrassed	Empathetic	Emptiness
Enchanted	Envy	Excitement
Fascinated	Fearful	Focused
Frazzled	Free	Friendly
Frustrated	Funny	Gloomy
Glum	Goofy	Grateful
Grieved	Guilt	Happiness
Hatred	Hatred	Heartbroken
Hopeful	Hopeless	Horrified
Horror	Horror	Humble
Hurting	Hysteria	Impatient
Infuriated	Insecure	Inspired
Insulted	Jealous	Joy
Kind	Lazy	Left out
Loathe	Lonely	Lost
Love	Lovesick	Loyal
Lust	Mean	Melancholy
Miserable	Misery	Needy
Nervous	Nostalgia	Obsessed
Offended	Optimistic	Outrage
Overwhelm	Panicked	Paranoid
Patient	Peace	Pensive
Pessimistic	Pity	Pity
Pride	Protective	Proud

List Of Common Emotions
Continued

Rage	Relief	Reluctant
Remorse	Resentful	Resentment
Resigned	Romantic	Sadness
Satisfaction	Self-pity	Sensual
Sentimental	Sexy	Shock
Shy	Skeptical	Sorrow
Spite	Stressed	Submissive
Sulkiness	Surprised	Suspicious
Sweet	Tender	Tense
Terrified	Tired	Troubled
Uncomfortable	Understanding	Uneasy
Unhappy	Vengeful	Vigilant
Vulnerable	Warm	Withdrawal
Wonder	Worn out	Worried
Wrath	Yearning	

Growing Your Emotional Awareness

No one likes to feel bad. We often try to push our feelings aside and overlook them. As children, we are often taught to *"suck it up," "walk it off,"* or *"just deal with it"* instead of acting on or expressing how we feel. When we ignore our emotions, they do not go away. The suppressed feelings instead intensify, causing them to fester and grow.

It takes a lot of internal energy to bury what we are sensing. Our effort to resist our emotions often backfires, drawing our attention to them counterproductively. We want things to be different. We want to feel different. We end up focusing on what we don't want, which only adds to the stress we already feel.

Whenever we are in a nerve-racking emotional place, rest assured our ego is in play. Our ego causes us to resist what our emotions call us to do. Thoughts like, *"I shouldn't have to do this,"* or *"Why is this happening to me?"* is a reflection of our ego rearing its ugly head, working to keep us where we are – in its clutches.

When the ego is activated, for some strange reason, we want to hang onto its opinion, its viewpoint, where we will draw a line in the sand and defend it forever. When situations like this occur, know you are attached to something important to the ego. Use it to transform your consciousness from oblivious to awareness. This will stop the ego right in its tracks.

When an unwanted emotion does arise, you can also use it to take stock of what is happening. Use the sensations you're feeling to learn more about yourself. For example, when you get angry, do you think someone is trying to take advantage of you? Do you feel they are belittling you? When you feel disappointed, what expectation did you have that was not met?

Sit with your feelings any time you feel uneasy. Notice them, observe them. Try to name them. Question their appearance. If you are feeling unhappy, investigate it. If you are feeling sad, reflect on it. What do your emotions have to say? If sad doesn't seem right, another emotion might encompass what you are experiencing more correctly.

You might also ask, *"What action do I need to take?"* Be open to the response you receive. You might feel compelled to take definitive steps. At other times, you might want to run and hide because what is being asked is too emotionally challenging to consider. You might also be guided to do nothing, and that is fine as well.

This might sound crazy, but the goal is not to change the emotion but allow it to be what it is. One of the best ways out of this conundrum is to befriend and accept your uncomfortable emotions. Acknowledge them and let them be. Even when you are in the depths of despair, remember your feelings are ever-changing. Their fleeting nature ensures that this too shall pass.

According to Frank Ostaseski, the author of the book *The Five Invitations*, *"The willingness to sit with fear IS an act of courage."* Accepting your downtrodden emotional state might be one of the bravest things you will ever do. Employ one of the tools we have already discussed, including deep breathing, being kind to yourself, tapping or journaling on a self-reflection question if they are particularly challenging and you are in doubt about what to do.

As your awareness grows, you might discover when a troubling feeling comes to the surface, you may begin viewing it not as a bummer but as an opportunity for growth. You might find yourself feeling grateful because this particular maladapted sentiment was brought to your attention. You might start detecting your destructive patterns as you take notice of your emotional state. This includes the behaviors you display or your unseen motives sitting in the background.

When you pay attention to how you feel, you will also discover where you focus your awareness the most. Is your focus on happiness, abundance, or inner peace, which will lead to feelings of positive expectations and joy, or is your attention on lack, fear, insecurity, or anger which can only lead to worry, pessimism, and depression? This can indicate the depth and breadth of your active neural pathways and some of your well-loved preprogrammed scripts.

Regardless of what your exploration reveals, this information can help you make better choices. You can use it to consciously decide whether to take action and change the situation, remove yourself from it, accept it, or stay where you are and be miserable. In the meantime, here are some questions you can use to reflect on your emotional state. Have a sense of curiosity and wonder as you journal about these items. What did you uncover?

Questions

What kind of mood am I in now?

What caused my current mood?

Where in my body am I noticing this emotion?

What thoughts are running through my mind?

Has this particular topic or subject arisen before?

What emotion got triggered?

What triggered this emotion?

Is there an internalized story tied to this situation that is amplifying my emotion?

What need, if any, is being met or needs to be met?

Is this need vital to me?

If I don't want 'X,' what do I want?

What is this emotion trying to communicate to me?

Is this emotion getting in my way of doing something?

What will I do differently the next time this emotion arises?

I want to bring up one last point when talking about observing emotions. Sometimes the emotions we are feeling are a false alarm. Something occurs and bounces off of one of our core beliefs, activating a trigger within us. Even though we may be aware of the stimulus, it does not mean our body will not react. At times like this, our ability to tolerate the emotion until it passes would be advised.

For example, you have abandonment issues, and a situation occurs where you are left feeling deserted. You can see nothing untoward occurred, yet you are triggered by it. By recognizing an old belief, an old wound, has been activated, it is easier to ride the storm out and allow all that has been rustled up within you to settle down.

We will go into greater depth about how to use our emotions to navigate our lives. Right now, our focus is on raising our awareness to what we are feeling in the first place.

Observing Our Behaviors

Our actions are readily observable. They are the outward reflection of our intentions. We would never take action if there were not a supporting thought and emotional reaction spurring us on. Our behaviors are often the first thing that cues us into a problem and lets us know something isn't right. Many of our actions are learned responses to situations. As they say in scientific circles, they are 'conditioned reflexes.'

Conditioned reflexes were first studied in the early 1900s by Ivan Pavlov. He discovered his dogs would salivate just before feeding. He introduced the playing of a metronome prior to food being distributed to the animals. The dogs quickly connected the sound of the metronome to the presentation of a tasty morsel. Their salivary glands, an unconscious bodily response, would activate even when food was not introduced. On some levels, we are all conditioned like Pavlov's dogs.

Following Pavlov's work, behavioral psychologists assumed all our actions are learned, conditioned, and ultimately repeated. When we are rewarded for displaying good, appropriate behaviors (positive reinforcement), we will respond to similar situations in the same way. When we receive negative reinforcement and are punished for behaving in an undesirable way, we shun the behavior. We learn at a young age what is proper to do as well as what we should avoid or suffer the consequences.

Some of the programming we receive, nevertheless, is misguided. Right, wrong or indifferent, we automatically follow our internalized scripts when we lack awareness. You see this in toxic, narcissistic people who were often incentivized even after displaying undesirable behaviors. Think of the screaming child who is given a toy as a means to quiet them down. They did not comply with the stated request but were rewarded anyway. As an adult, these individuals will melt down or have a temper tantrum if they don't get their way. Why? Because they know, based on their life experiences, they can wear you down and reap the benefit if they persist.

What about all of the things you are taught to steer clear of as a child, be it overtly or covertly. *"Don't pick your nose." "Don't talk to strangers." "Don't cry." "Don't talk back."* Regardless of the messaging, the net result is that you will respond to similar situations, real or imagined, in a parallel way. You are reenacting an old script to get something you want or to avoid something uncomfortable.

The Power Of Choice

A certain amount of nervousness ensues when we find ourselves in a difficult situation. A healthy individual might take steps to deal with a problem directly. They might say what is on their minds, uphold a boundary or communicate their needs. Our programming, however, can cause us to act in unhealthy, non-self-preserving ways. These limiting behaviors stop us from relieving the uneasiness felt inside. This will only escalate the moroseness we are sensing, making it near impossible to find a positive solution. These unhealthy behaviors may offer some relief, but when they become a consistent subconscious response to obstacles, they can create even bigger problems.

Regardless of what happens to us throughout our lives, we do and always have a choice. We can choose to unlearn destructive behaviors and replace them with better, healthier ones. When detrimental scripts control our lives, we display 'akrasia.' Akrasia is the act of going against our own better judgment. It is when everything inside us tells us to do something, but we do not take our best interest to heart and follow through on the action.

Procrastination is a perfect example of akrasia. We might want to lose weight, quit smoking, clean our house, or find a new job, yet we don't move forward to accomplish our goal. We know what we want to do; we just don't, and then we suffer from the anxiety we feel inside. Procrastination tends to activate our inner critic, so instead of the joy of a job well done, we beat ourselves up for our failure.

One of my clients, Emily, is a breast cancer survivor. She was prescribed Tamoxifen to reduce the risk of the cancer recurring. One of the side effects of Tamoxifen is its impact on bone mineral density. Woman, who take it, are advised to supplement their diet with calcium, magnesium, and vitamin D to prevent osteoporosis.

I love Emily, but she is a chronic worrier. One of the things she would be constantly concerned about was her bone density. She would admit to not taking the recommended supplements and regularly panicked about potential bone loss. After months of addressing her fear of developing osteoporosis, I stated the obvious out loud.

I believed all of Emily's concerns would disappear if she took the daily bone support. I suggested that her failure to do what she knew she should be doing created all of the worries in the first place. She could take the pills as required and be stress-free, or she could avoid them and continue worrying. Emily went for option number one, and we have not talked about bone density again.

Sometimes it can be that easy. We can simply make a different decision. Then all the stress, worry, and anxiety we are feeling vanishes. Just like that!

Akrasia And Enkrateia

According to author and researcher Josh Kaufman, *"Akrasia has four general parts: a task, a desire/want, a "should," and emotional experience of resistance."* In changing our inner world, the resistance we experience is most often the hardest part to overcome. This resistance is bound up with our ego and our subconscious programs. It is what creates the confusion, chaos, and agitation we feel.

When we take action we experience the pleasurable feeling of *"It's done, over with. I can put this behind me and move on."* There might also be times when our resistance is so overwhelming we make the unhealthy choice anyway, even if we have time to reflect. The pleasure? It was easier than challenging the underlying programming that was creating the resistance in the first place.

There could be other factors involved as well. Maybe you are addicted to the stress hormone cortisol. The world might not seem right, normal, when your body is depleted of this fight or flight activating hormone. Perhaps the thought of making a different choice brings up subconscious memories of negative consequences. You may have been taught to give up your power, your autonomy over yourself and accept whatever is being handed to you, no questions asked. Any of these can cause us to ignore ourselves.

'Enkrateia' is the opposite of akrasia. It is that act of taking our power back. It allows us to assume control of the wheel. Sometimes the choices we make are easy, and at other times they might take every bit of gumption we have to move forward with them. They can frighten us to the core, but a part of us recognizes the selection we make, hard as it may be, is ultimately in our best interest. You never know. The option you pick may seem off-putting on the surface, but it is, in reality, creating space for something new and wondrous to arise.

Ending a relationship, for example, at times might be easy. *"See ya! Got to go!"* It can be the hardest thing we will ever do at other times. It might trigger our need to feel safe or our fear of being alone. It might activate our abandonment wounds or cause us to wonder how we will care for ourselves. Even in situations where our inner world is going crazy, and our inner critic is running on overdrive, we can allow our critical thinking to step forward and remind us how unhealthy the relationship is and finally say the word *"good-bye."* I'm sure some breathing would be involved.

The self-programming nature of our subconscious mind makes this all possible. We are not doomed to live with the scripts embedded in us early on. We can change our behaviors by creating new programs or revising the old ones. What was once a nail-biting experience can become something where the blood doesn't run out of our face the next time we try it. We might discover our choice resulted in a positive experience, even though, at the time, it felt scary as all get out. Each time we act out a new behavior, it will be easier and the next time even easier. We might even reach a point where we naturally and automatically respond using this newfound skill.

Making Lasting Behavioral Changes

You might be wondering where to start this process. It all starts with monitoring your actions and paying attention to your feelings. As part of your burgeoning awareness practice, you may have detected a few behaviors that are unproductive, unhealthy, or even toxic to yourself. Perhaps you storm out of a room when you get upset, start to yell and scream when you feel frustrated, or clam up when put on the spot. You may have concluded that this is not how you want to deal with problems. Once a behavioral issue is identified, steps can be taken to change it.

Sometimes a behavior is really just a bad habit. You have gotten used to doing certain things in certain ways which are not beneficial to you. These habits, if worked on, are relatively easy to change. You simply have to decide to take an alternative action, even if the deed seems repulsive, disagreeable, boring, or creates tension inside of you. Be present as you engage in these activities. Do them with a mindful sense of alertness. You might unknowingly discover a sense of enjoyment where your conscious mind could only register irritation before.

Other behaviors may be overcharged with emotional energy. The thought of performing it, or in some cases avoiding it, may cause your inner world to be consumed with intrusive thoughts. Your stress response system may activate, causing you to want to fight, run or freeze. Don't beat yourself up for the reaction you initially have. Just notice it, and be mindful of it the best you can.

Changing our behaviors is a process. It often happens in three stages. Observation of troubling behaviors is the first phase and is vital when wanting to make long-lasting adjustments in how we act. Observations can include: What is the problematic behavior? What is the chain of events that leads to the unwanted behavior? What typically happens when it appears? How do I feel inside when it occurs?

While in the observation phase, there isn't any requirement to take a new or different approach. You are just looking, noticing, and becoming aware of what is. What you are doing, what you are feeling, and what you are thinking during these moments? If you find yourself like a deer in the headlights as you try to assess your motives, it happens to the best of us. Breathe!

Our focus right now is on the behavior itself. You may act in a certain way when you are with specific people or when a particular emotion is triggered. A bad day at work could be the common denominator, or it might only crop up when you drink. Regardless, it all starts with observation.

I wish I could tell you each stage only lasts a week or two, but they unfold in their own time and in their own manner. Use this time to learn about yourself. Trust me, given enough observation, it is only a matter of time before you become sick and tired of the old undesirable behavior, and you will automatically move into the next phase.

The second phase is the testing phase. In phase 2, you must be willing to step outside your comfort zone, where you have felt safe and cozy, perhaps, in a dysfunctional way, for years. This is where you get to test out a new action by trying something different. Maybe you expressed and held a boundary with a friend. Perhaps you said *"No"* for the first time ever. You left a party, got off the phone, or ended a conversation because it didn't feel good to you, whereas, in the past, you would have stayed until the bitter end.

Taking the chance and acting based on your new information can be one of the hardest things you will ever do. I remember the first time I confronted someone and plainly expressed my needs. I felt like I was having a panic attack when I hung up the phone. Deep down, I knew I was doing the right thing but was a bit surprised at the upheaval I felt when all was said and done.

If discomfort arises, use these thoughts and emotions to your advantage. Confront your inner critic and acknowledge your old programming coming to the surface. You might feel like a failure. You might want to throw in the towel and quit. Guilt may surface. You might question your decision to act differently and wonder if your internal rules are flawed. Obligation may cause you to second guess your judgment. You might cave in and go back on your initial decision.

You didn't fail. You did it, or at least tried. That is the crucial part! Focus on your efforts rather than the net results. You are learning and growing. Love and honor yourself regardless of how things play out. Enjoy the bumpy road you are on and the stage of growth you are in. You are in the testing phase, practicing a new behavior and observing the results. You are creating a new path, not the right path or the wrong path, a new one. Even if the choice you make seems uncomfortable, suspend your judgment.

Notice it, pay attention to it, challenge it. See how deep the rabbit hole goes. Use your reaction as a measuring stick to gauge your resistance level or the power the negative programming has over you. Remember, someone, somewhere, impressed upon you these notions, and you have been living by them and acting them out for years. The saying doesn't go, *"If, at first, you don't succeed – you are a failure."* It says, *"Try, try again."*

On the flip side, once you exhibit the new behavior, you might discover you can breathe easier, your mind has stopped racing, your body has begun to relax, or your intrusive thoughts have calmed down. Notice that as well. What does it feel like in your body? Revel in the sensation. Your new behavior might also elicit a response in situations which involve other people. Was it a positive response or a negative one? Notice that too.

As time passes and you become more experienced, you may discover times when you respond to a situation on autopilot and revert to your old ways. Use these little slip-ups to evaluate the 'before you' and your inner state and the 'new you' and your updated internal state. You are seeing firsthand the impact your old choices have had on your life and the benefits you are now experiencing using your new, more conscious ones.

Congratulate yourself on the massive steps you have made to date. Take a moment and pat yourself on the back for catching your backslide. Hopefully, you will see the error of your ways and challenge yourself to do better in the future. Don't judge yourself. Accept it as part of the learning process. How would you ever have known your healthy choices felt so good if you didn't occasionally make an unhealthy one?

Like the first phase, the second part of the change process can take some time. You didn't learn to walk on your first try, and this is the same. Give yourself permission to fail. Learn the lesson from it and move on. Refrain from letting a few blunders or failed attempts ruin your progress and commitment to yourself.

The third phase of this process often slides in unnoticed. It is usually only perceivable in hindsight. One day you may realize you no longer exhibit the unwanted behavior, or the number of times you've fallen off the wagon has dramatically diminished.

Well done! You have entered the third phase and are on your way to embracing your new behavior as an active script in your psyche. Just think about all of the new neural pathways you have created in the process.

Getting Over Myself

I was timid growing up. It took a lot for me to feel safe and open up to a new person. I was not too fond of the fact I was scared to talk to strangers. More often than not, my words would get caught in my throat, unable to escape the tight grip being held over them. When I did try to exert myself, I would get triggered and dissociate. That would surely put a nail in the *"I'm not saying a damn thing"* coffin. It bothered me so much I knew I had to fix it. I wasn't sure how, but I was determined to try.

I made a commitment to work on this after I moved to California. I found a job shortyly after my arrival and would walk to work daily. En route, I would regularly stop at the local convenience store. It was hard for me not to notice my troubling behavior. I discovered I was even afraid to talk to the clerk behind the counter. How sad is that? This observation did, however, cause me to conjure up a plan.

I decided one morning to say *"hi"* to the cashier before she greeted me. You are probably thinking, *"That doesn't sound very hard."* Well, let me tell you, I was terrified. The first time I tried it, I literally stopped outside the store and took several deep breaths before walking in. I managed to squeak out a meager *"hi"* and went about my business. My heart was racing, and my body was shaking with the utterance of that one simple word.

It has taken me years of working on this behavior to see measurable results. People who know me now are often shocked to discover I was ever shy.

One of the things I've noticed recently is how certain situations bring up my old programming forcing my mouth closed. It primarily appears when expressing my needs to others. Just the thought of speaking my truth shuts me down and sends me into a period of intrusive thoughts and runaway rumination.

I started paying attention to times when I was battling intrusive thoughts. My plan? When they were detected, I was to bite the bullet and say something – out loud. There was an interesting outcome to this approach: my ruminating stopped. So when I have found myself in this place, I would say to myself, *"Just freaking do it."* Sometimes I could, and apparently, at other times, I was not very successful.

My communication trigger reared its ugly head again recently. A very close friend and I had a weekly girls' night out. One day she informed me she wanted to permanently change the day of our outing. My automatic reaction was to respond, *"Okay."* I went home and started ruminating about it. It really bothered me. I didn't want to change the day and to be honest, there wasn't any discussion about it. She decided, which set off old feelings of not having a choice and another old script of having to accept what was handed to me.

My rumination continued for a while, and even though we would see each other, I said nothing. Based on how much I thought about it, I knew I needed to say something, but I could not confront her. A few weeks after the change, she brought the subject up – thank God. She asked if I was good with the change. I shared with her I was not, adding I felt left out of the decision-making process. She wondered why I hadn't said anything, and I confessed I was unable to. There was so much fear inside the idea of saying something was terrifying. This left me incapable of moving forward and expressing my thoughts.

That was a big hello to me and gave me yet another opportunity to look at and address this deeply ingrained toxic program that has plagued me my whole life.

I keep talking about how modifying our inner world is a practice. Well, I'm still working on this one and look forward to the next opportunity to implement more conscious, healthy communication behaviors, especially when I detect resistance in my body. I am crossing my fingers that when a similar situation presents itself, it will be easier for me to express myself and not find myself white-knuckling a chair, forcing myself to say what is on my mind, or making the unhealthy *Akrasia* decision to say nothing at all.

Journaling can help accelerate this practice. As I mentioned earlier, journaling is the process of documenting your thoughts, emotions, ideas, beliefs, and motivations. It can be instrumental if you have difficulty tapping into the associated thoughts or feelings tied to unwanted behaviors. Here are some questions you can ask yourself as you work to change.

Questions

What pattern or behavior did I display?

How was I feeling when it happened?

Why did I do it? What was the underlying cause?

What needs are being met as I engage in this behavior?

How is this behavior impacting my life?

What positive behavior can I use to replace the negative one?

What could I have done differently in this situation?

What is keeping me from taking a more healthy action?

What do I think will happen if I do something different?

What small change can I make next time I notice this pattern wanting to play out?

An Exercise For My Procrastinator Friends

Are you someone who puts off doing projects consistently? Well then, this exercise is for you! Pick one disagreeable task to focus on. Have you wanted to clean your closets, paint a room or weed your garden? Every day or once a week, spend some time working on it. Identify the quantity of work you would like to accomplish or designate a specific amount of time to the performance of the endeavor and then do it.

Eckhart Tolle suggests, *"When you do things, do them with joy in your heart. If you cannot feel joy, do it with acceptance. It is something that I have to do now, and I do it willingly. If you feel neither and cannot get neutral to doing something, then perhaps you should stop. Peace comes when you surrender your actions. The surrender can fill you with aliveness and perhaps even joy in what you are doing. This simple shift will increase your ability to enjoy what you do and improve the overall quality of your life."*

Please don't consider it an unwanted, undeserved, and dreadful chore. View it as spending time loving yourself. In a short while, you will begin to see progress. Before you know it, the project will be done. Revel in your small successes and celebrate a job well done when you complete it. You will also discover that the part of you that has been hounding you to take care of it will disappear. You will be able to stop beating yourself up over it. It will be done and no longer hanging over your head.

Changing Our Automatic Thoughts

We do not appreciate the importance of maintaining positive thoughts. Positive thoughts lead to good, uplifting feelings. Negative thoughts lead to uncomfortable or painful ones. We all struggle with harmful or ineffective thinking, especially when things go wrong. Once we are in a low mood, the flow of negative ideas entering our minds can seem unstoppable. Researchers suggest some people are more prone to negative thinking, but as we learned earlier, the reality is, we are all plagued by them.

What if you could change your thoughts? What impact would it have? According to self-help author Wayne Dyer, changing your thoughts can change your life. It all comes down to paying attention to and controlling our mental state. It is generally believed having no thoughts at all is better than having negative ones. In turn, trying to force ourselves into having a positive one doesn't always produce successful results. The more we strive to stop harmful thoughts from entering our minds they typically come back with a vengeance.

One solution to this predicament is to take a few deep breaths, become mindful of your thoughts, and work on bringing yourself back into the present moment. Being in the present moment helps us let go of our resistance. Our negative thoughts will begin to fade away and fall to the wayside. By changing our focus we can stop intrusive thinking right in their tracks.

The 17-Second Rule

One of the most powerful tools I have encountered to tackle and overcome negative thinking comes from the work of Ester Hicks, who channels a spiritual being called Abraham. Abraham puts forward the concept of the '17 second rule'. The 17-second rule is similar to the 5-second rule. Many of us employ the 5-second rule when a piece of food falls to the floor. This rule permits us to use the slightly tainted item as long as it's picked up within 5 seconds.

The 17-second rule works in much the same way. Its purpose is to help us take control of our thoughts by distracting us from something unwanted and replacing it with dead air or, better yet, something positive. The belief is after 17 seconds, a new negative thought will enter our awareness and then another. Each new thought adds to the forward momentum being experienced. We never have just one unsettling, intrusive thought if left unchecked. We have one, and then another, and then another until we find ourselves camping out in our rabbit hole.

When I first heard of the 17-second rule, I wasn't sure if it would work, but I was feeling pretty desperate and decided I would try it. I began using it when I got rid of 'Mr. Right' and was working on rebuilding my life. Whenever my mind wandered off to ruminate about him, I would stop, breathe and try to think about something else.

At first, I could only divert my focus for a few minutes, but as time passed, I found I was less drawn to thinking about our fractured relationship. And trust me. There were days when I constantly reminded myself, *"17-second rule, 17-second rule."* I have found this tool so effective I utilize it whenever I find myself entertaining negative, critical, or unhealthy thoughts. When I start to worry, or when my anxiety flares, I 17-second rule it. It has been a game-changer for me.

As I practiced this technique, I discovered I would no longer end up in my rabbit hole when noxious thoughts crossed my mind. One day I surprisingly noticed I was not standing on the precipice of the hole any longer, but it was somehow 'over there.' Since starting with this technique, I have not visited my rabbit hole once, and I must tell you, I do not miss it AT ALL!

For the 17-second rule to work, you have to change the channel in your mind from the horror movie that might be going on inside to something else, something better. This creates a gap and interrupts the flow of your thoughts. Any mindfulness tool can be used to shift your mental focus.

You can also do this by recalling a happy moment in your life, thinking about a beloved pet, or by looking around and taking in the beauty of your location. At times this method worked great for me, and at other times, coming up with a happy thought, thinking about something I was looking forward to, or, God forbid, finding something to be thankful for was beyond my reach.

This would cause me to resort to a contingency plan where I would find something physical to do: dust, wash dishes, clean a bathroom, wash the floors, rake leaves, mow the yard, or weed my garden. If done with focused intention, these activities will give you something else to think about. They can also help you burn off the excess emotional energy you might be carrying in your body, helping you to let it go. My house was immaculate early on.

Challenging Your Inner Critic

We've already talked about our inner critic. We never feel good or uplifted when we interact with it. We only end up feeling down. Maybe your inner critic is very active and opinionated, and it goes on and on with its non-stop hateful chatter. Regardless of its activity level, I'll bet you are wondering what you can do to get it to stop.

Like our negative thinking, have you ever tried to force your inner critic to quit ranting? Its voice only becomes louder and more incessant the more you struggle. Lay down your weapons, and instead of fighting it, start paying attention to this unwanted voice in your head.

Does it talk to you all of the time, or does it step forward when specific situations are encountered? When it starts, do your emotions follow, where you find yourself moving quickly into a bad place? What is it saying to you?

You can challenge the comments your inner critic shares. Ask it why it keeps saying these hurtful things to you. Then you can decide whether you agree with it or not. Here are some questions you can ask yourself when your inner critic shows itself.

Questions

What is your inner critic saying to you? Have you heard these words before?

How does it make you feel when it speaks to you this way?

How do you usually respond when your inner critic speaks up?

What was going on when it got activated?

How can you love, honor, and respect yourself more when it becomes active?

I Am!

The 17-second rule works excellent in stopping our inner critic from running on overdrive, but another thought-shifting method I like using when my inner critic is berating me is called the 'I Am' Exercise. Like all of the exercises I have suggested, the I Am exercise is simple to use. All you need do is say to yourself, or out loud, positive things you believe about yourself.

This practice will bring you back into the present moment when focused on. It has a second benefit. It reminds you of your positive characteristics, which support your self-worth, your self-confidence, and your self-esteem. What could be better than telling yourself how awesome you really are? Inner critic be damned.

If I were to make an I Am list for myself, statements I would include are:

- I am strong
- I am confident
- I am smart
- I am funny
- I am a hard worker
- I am pragmatic
- I am motivated
- I am conscientious
- I am successful in my endeavors

Other words you could use are: loving, giving, caring, committed, abundant, radiant, enthusiastic, peaceful, tranquil, or serene. Go with what feels right to you.

As you make each statement, breathe into it. Pay attention to how it makes you feel inside. Become aware of your growing inner strength as you remind yourself how much you rock this world.

It is essential to be careful to not use words that are not true about who you are and your reality. For example, using the statement, *"I am rich,"* opens the door for my inner critic to jump in and remind me just how much I am lacking in this area. This will only serve to bring your energy down, so choose wisely.

Digging To The Core

In time, you might begin noticing a pattern to what your inner critic says. It tell you the same things over and over again. You're a failure, fat, lazy, or stupid. This pattern of negative commentary can be used to identify limiting and embedded core beliefs you have about yourself. We all have limiting beliefs that control our thoughts and our lives. They have been part of us for so long that we often don't recognize them when they come to the surface.

We can take the negative commentary being presented to us and put a positive spin on it. If your inner critic suggests you are a terrible mother, turn it around and state, *"I'm doing the best I can to raise my children."* It might remind you of how you are a failure. You can flip the script and state, *"It's okay to make mistakes."* These short uplifting statements are considered affirmations. Affirmations are positive phrases you can repeat throughout the day. They are designed to transform negative thoughts while strengthening your positive thinking.

I don't know, and maybe I am complaining, but I never found affirmations effective. When I read affirmations such as *"I'm enthusiastic and excited about my work,"* or *"I radiate love, and others reflect love back to me,"* or even *"each day of my life is filled with abundance,"* my mind immediately goes *"yea, yea, yea, right."*

Statements such as these, ones that do not resonate with my current view of myself activate my inner critic. Perhaps I have not spent enough time repeating the sayings to allow this practice a chance to work. For me, keeping my inner critic at bay seems more important.

Nonetheless, I am bringing up affirmations in this context because Sondra Ray, in her book *I Deserve Love*, offers the following very powerful exercise that relies on affirmations to dig deep into a core belief. This exercise brings the negative thoughts and feelings stored in our subconscious mind to the surface. It allows us to transmute them into a newfound understanding of ourselves.

The basis of the affirmation should be a declaration your inner critic keeps bringing up. This statement should be changed into an upbeat version of it. *"I don't matter"* can be modified to *"I matter."* Use *"I'm proud of myself and my achievements"* instead of *"I'm a failure."* *"I suck"* can be replaced with *"I love and accept myself."*

Write the positive affirmation down on a piece of paper. Jot down whatever appears in your mind below it. Keep writing down the affirmation, documenting what comes to the surface until you feel the energy change, clear, shift, become lighter, or leaves you feeling complete.

This exercise was beyond powerful the first time I did it. I was amazed at how many hurtful thoughts and supercharged emotions bubbled up. I felt drained and exhausted when I was done, and even though I felt uncomfortable, I knew I had achieved a breakthrough. Below is an actual session I did regarding one of my core beliefs. What would my inner critic constantly say? *"Well, such and such and such and such happened because I'm broken."* After working through this process, I do not think I am broken anymore.

Digging To The Core Example

I Am Not Broken
> *Oh, yes, you are! Think about when...*

I Am Not Broken
> *Well, if you are not broken, then who can we blame?*

I Am Not Broken
> *I was never broken. You wanted too much and put me into situations I could not emotionally handle.*

I Am Not Broken
> *Wait! Look at all of these people who think you are.*

I Am Not Broken
> *I'm scared.*

I Am Not Broken
> *But everyone says it's true.*

I Am Not Broken
> *I am having a hard time believing it is true.*

I Am Not Broken
> *If I believe it is true, then that means there is something wrong with 'them.'*

I Am Not Broken
> *Why do you have to blame me for everything?*

I Am Not Broken
> *You are a horrible person. That hurts!*

I Am Not Broken
> *I just want you to love me and see value in me, but you don't. You only see yourself.*

I Am Not Broken

> *How could you do that? How could you emotionally devastate someone like that?*

I Am Not Broken
> *They could not feel my pain.*

I Am Not Broken
> *I do not have to vibrate at that energy. I do not have to live surrounded by their pain and hate.*

I Am Not Broken
> *I can live to the beat of my own drummer.*

I Am Not Broken
> *I am sorry if you do not like it.*

I Am Not Broken
> *I am not broken, and I forgive myself for believing their sorry selves.*

I Am Not Broken
> *You can't use it to hold me down and dim my light anymore.*

I Am Not Broken
> *Amen. I am not!*

Putting Our Stories To Rest

While our thoughts might engulf us in a sea of negativity, they do not hurt or cause us pain. They are the initiating spark that sends our inner world into motion. We can have a thought which will set off a torrent of emotions and potentially send us into a downward spiral, while at other times, we can have a similar thought and not even lift an eyebrow. It all depends on our interpretation.

It is not a situation that causes us to be happy or unhappy; it is our thoughts about it. It is the stories we tell ourselves that shape our perception of the world. We will not activate a painful emotional response if we change our opinion and interpretation of a triggering event. Yes, we can change how our emotions show up when we pay attention to and do not buy into the dramatic, awe-inspiring, unconstructive stories we tell ourselves.

We often assume our feelings provide us with true and accurate information, but this might not always be the case. Our emotions signal us to pay attention to something. That's it. More likely than not, the story we tell ourselves is what precipitates a painful emotional response. Remember Matti's mom, who went off the deep end when Matti did not come home at the designated time? Her mind went on overdrive, where she told herself all kinds of dreadful tales.

When we change our internal narrative and rewrite the story, we change our emotional response. Maybe this has happened to you. Your boyfriend is talking to and smiling at an attractive, unknown woman at a work-related party. Your impression of their encounter is he is flirting with her. Right on cue, your negative thinking jumps in, and you start worrying if your other half is being unfaithful. You give in to the activated negative thought. Feelings of jealousy arise. *"That low-down dirty scoundrel,"* you might be saying to yourself.

Try to catch yourself in those moments. Challenge your automatic thoughts by taking a step back and evaluating the facts. Your boyfriend is talking to someone of the opposite sex. Fact. There are a lot of people from his job at this get-together. Fact. Could she be a coworker talking about an upcoming project, or are they gossiping about someone? Maybe. Perhaps they worked together in the past, and he hasn't seen her in a long time, and they are catching up. That could be true too. This slight mindful pause may allow healthier, less noxious thoughts to enter your awareness.

You might also be able to stop the distasteful narrative before it moves through your mind as you raise your awareness. Breathe, think a happy thought. Imagine catching yourself early on and recognizing what you are doing. You are in storytelling mode. A slight shift of focus can be all it takes to prevent you from entering a downward spiral and help you to move into a more neutral place.

I have to admit identifying our stories can be a bit challenging, but it is soooooo easy to observe it in other people as they spin tragic yarns about their lives. It can be illuminating, yet sad to watch as they enter into the grips of their own negative thinking. In this vein, you might want to find someone willing to help you identify when you have moved from fact to fiction. That's right. Find a storytelling buddy.

Ask them to reflect back to you when you have mentally shifted gears and have started relaying an untruthful internal narrative. Create an agreement between you and your friend in which they have permission to point out when you have engaged in this bad habit. This will help raise your awareness of the false tales you are telling yourself. Hopefully, this trick will help you become cognizant of this unhealthy behavior and assist you in changing it.

Just a FYI. I have tried to raise the awareness of friends when they are in the midst of their stories. Someone hell-bent on crashing and burning in emotional flames, the act of bringing up the notion they may be telling themselves lies doesn't work very well. In any case, I am throwing in a few questions you can use to reflect on any stories you might be telling yourself.

Questions

What is this thought based on?

Is this thought really true?

Did I interpret this situation correctly?

Is there any proof to support the accuracy of this thought?

Is there another way this information could be interpreted?

What's the worst thing that could happen?

What would I do if the worst thing did happen?

Quit Your Kvetching

I want to delve into one last concept before we move on. Would you believe the average person complains (kvetches) 10-30 times a day? Neither did I. I always thought people complained as a way to vent, get things off their chest, or unburden themselves of their frustrations. Complainers will share their tales of woe, letting you know how hard life is, how things didn't go their way, or how unlucky they are. They are usually happy to share every unbearable, intolerable, or disastrous thing that has happened to them.

The truth of the matter is we'll gripe about anything under the sun if given the chance. We whine about our aches and pains, our jobs, the weather, poor customer service, traffic, spam phone calls, and bad wifi connections. It is easy to rant and rave about the things in our lives that aren't working, but complaining serves no purpose other than to further entrench us into our own negative thinking.

People, who constantly complain, by–in–large, are always unhappy. They might be surrounded by success but are unable to enjoy the fruits that life offers. Their focus is always on the downbeat, depressing lack they are experiencing. They have a perpetual glass-half-empty mentality toward life.

Each time we find fault with someone or something, we strengthen the negative neural pathways in our brains. This makes it easier and easier for us to overlook the good we encounter and only see the bad. With all of the harmful thinking we do, it makes sense that we are all a bunch of complainers living in a society of complainers.

Will Bowen, author of *A Complaint Free World*, identifies five primary reasons people kvetch.

- People oddly complain as a way to connect with others. We might gripe about the bad weather or the slowness of service as a way to start a conversation.

- Some people complain about others to show their pre-eminence. They might make comments like *"Oh, he is a litterbug"* or *"She shouldn't drive that way,"* both of which imply the complainer's thoughts on a matter are superior, and they know a better way of doing things.
- Some people use complaining as a way to control others. They will use their toxic words to badmouth or minimize an opponent and strengthen their status and position by diminishing others.
- Complaining can be used to evade responsibility and avoid taking action. Often when you offer a suggestion to help improve these individual's situation, they will automatically find fault with your idea and moan about that as well.
- Others use it as an excuse for their poor performance, their destructive behaviors, or for not taking action. They might complain about congested traffic as they show up late or how they didn't get a good night's sleep as a cover for why they aren't prepared for a meeting.

One reason Will Bowen doesn't offer is: complaining can be a learned behavior. Children who grow up in an environment where complaining is the rule and not the exception will find it a natural part of their lives. I come from a family of professional kvetchers, so I come by complaining as a pastime honestly.

I started noticing this active pattern right after I started paying attention to my negative thinking. I was shocked to detect how much I complained. And believe me, I was good at it. Some of the best and funniest stories I tell are of me complaining about something. Once I recognized the telltale signs of my own whining, I knew it had to go, especially if it was getting in the way of me being happy.

Recognizing and becoming conscious of your negative thinking is the first step to unraveling this process. If you weren't thinking negatively in the first place, you wouldn't have anything to grumble about. At first, you may start to notice the eyes of the person you are talking to glaze over while you are speaking. They might seem like they want the conversation to end and run from your presence before you can get into another one of your woeful tales.

In time, you might start to catch yourself in the process of complaining as you put your attention on this behavior. Unfortunately, once started, it is nearly impossible to put that genie back in the bottle and stop the flow of negative words coming out of our mouths. And again, that's okay. Finish what you are saying and make a mental note of it. All you can do is try to do better the next time. As your thoughts shift from negativity to being more positive, you will find you will not have anything to complain about.

Killing The Kvetch

Want to kill the kvetch? Then perhaps it is time to develop an 'attitude of gratitude.' Gratitude is identified as both a mood and an emotion. It is one emotion we have conscious control over. We express gratitude when we acknowledge and appreciate the moments, skills, people, places, and things that bring us pleasure. Our happiness quotient automatically increases when we feel thankful for who we are and what we have. It is the antithesis of complaining.

Gratitude helps us spotlight the positive aspects of our lives. The conscious effort of articulating our appreciation magnifies the sensation of good feelings in our bodies. You might already express gratitude when you take your first sip of coffee in the morning. Or what about when you lucked out and got one of those up-close parking spots at a crowded mall? I know I always say *"thank you."*

There is so much more we can be thankful for in our lives, much of which we overlook. We can stop and appreciate the peacefulness of a serene forest. We can be grateful for our health. We can be appreciative of a task someone graciously did for us.

We can even be thankful for bad experiences or negative encounters, particularly if we learn a lesson from them or can decipher their underlying message. Bottom line, we can begin a practice of paying attention and cherishing the small things in our lives that bring us joy.

People who count their blessings tend to be happier and experience more positive emotions. Gratitude trains the brain to be more optimistic, strengthening our positive neural circuits. You can't complain while embracing gratitude. It is a great tool to use to shift our focus from being a downer to one of contentment. Imagine, instead of griping, you automatically find something within a situation to be grateful for? Hallelujah, praise the Lord. All you need do is say *"thank you."*

Exercise

Give it a try. You can begin by thinking of three things you are thankful for each day. When my children were young, we would go around the kitchen table and share what we were grateful for over dinner. No kids? Find a gratitude buddy, someone you can practice gratitude with. Some people suggest having a gratitude journal where you spend a little time each day or week writing down what you are grateful for.

Final Thoughts

So what did you decide to focus on first? Did you begin by observing your self-talk, the manifestation of your core beliefs, or the expectations put in place by your ego? Perhaps you focused on your behaviors so you can understand why you do the things you do, your hidden motives and your subconscious triggers. You may have started by raising your awareness to the never-ending stream of emotions within and began exploring what they are trying to tell you.

Who knows, you may have decided to cultivate the habit of looking for the silver lining in the situations you encounter or commenced by letting go of your preconceived expectations of people and events. Your first step might have been to stop promoting your traditional 'worst than' attitude. Your focus may have been on quieting your inner critic, or quitting your kvetching. Where your set off on this journey is totally up to you, but regardless of where you begin, awareness is the key to change.

The Superconscious Mind

"The lies are always loud. The Truth is always quiet."

- Mal

Did you know you can take your transformation even further by actively engaging your superconscious mind? As you may recall, we compared the subconscious mind to a computer hard drive loaded with our thoughts, impressions, judgments, memories, and beliefs. It comes complete with artificial intelligence programs, which operate in the background. These programs can be activated consciously or unconsciously, where they can trigger emotional responses or rote behaviors. We have trained our onboard computers to view and respond to life through our life experiences. This has allowed us to live on autopilot, never in control and never truly happy.

Our superconscious mind operates on a completely different set of principles. Our superconscious mind exists above our thoughts, emotions, and active programs. It is not automatic and does not come with preprogrammed scripts installed. You have to make an effort to tap into it and access the wonders it holds. Would exploring it be worth it if it supported your ability to be happier, more content, and joyful in your everyday experiences?

The superconscious is the least understood aspect of our inner world, yet we have all experienced our superconscious mind at work. Maybe you didn't realize you were interacting with it. We are accessing the superconscious when we have moments of raised awareness, in times when we feel good, relaxed, and connected to the world around us. Having a 'light bulb' moment, those times when the answer to an elusive problem suddenly enters our awareness is the work of the superconscious. The writer, painter, poet, or musician, who feels inspired by their craft, regularly taps into this source.

The superconscious connects us with an infinite source of wisdom and inspiration. It is where true creativity is found. It allows us to bring forth information without the encumbrances of our ego or inner critic. When we have moments of increased awareness, they seem spontaneous and outside of our conscious control. They just happen. These instances of clarity do not need to be hit or miss. We can learn how to access this elevated plane whenever we want to.

The idea of the superconscious is still hotly debated among scholars. Scientists like Sigmund Freud, the father of modern psychology, believed our mind only consists of conscious and unconscious planes. Some discount the existence of the superconscious entirely, while others claim when you introduce the idea of the superconscious into the discussion of the mind, you are *"bringing religion into psychology."*

As I was researching this section, I found it fascinating how far more is discussed regarding our negative states of being than any positive ones. Concise volumes have been written on every conceivable aberration of negativity. Rarely is the concept of the superconscious discussed much less explored by mainstream researchers. I was dumbfounded that the scientific community didn't have more to say about it.

Those who do explore the principles tied to the superconscious customarily come from religious, spiritual, and metaphysical traditions. To my astonishment, feeling good is relegated to the writings of the saints, profits, and mystics. It is largely ignored by mental health professionals who corner the market on feeling good.

The lack of information from mainstream scientific sources leaves me in an awkward position. It is much easier and a whole lot less controversial to talk about neural pathways with a diverse audience. To continue with our conversation, I am forced to utilize words and ideas that may seem palatable to some and taboo to others.

It is not my intention to push religious or spiritual concepts on anyone. My goal is to investigate the working of our inner world, yet, to move forward, I have no choice but to tread down this path. So please forgive me in advance for the terminology I will use to convey these topics. As you read on, I believe you will recognize the workings of the superconscious in your daily life, regardless of the verbiage used.

The primary concern of most religious and spiritual traditions is to develop a relationship with the higher levels of existence that sits behind conscious reality. People who speak of tapping into source, their higher self, the collective conscious, the universe, or the universal mind are referring to an infinite source of wisdom they can access external to their physical being. When people feel one with the divine, God, Jesus, or the Holy Spirit, they too, are alluding to this mysterious connection that is available to each of us. Fostering our relationship with the superconscious, the universe, source, our higher self, God, Jesus, the Holy Spirit, or whatever word you want to use, is how we are going to shift our focus from the clutches of the ego to something bigger and better than ourselves.

You do not have to be religious or spiritual or become a devotee to pursue a relationship with the divine. It doesn't require you to go to church, say a rosary, climb a mountain, or chant. You don't even have to become a vegetarian to connect with this unseen force.

The mechanisms we will be delving into are already built into each and every one of us. All it entails is for you to quiet your mind, look inside and raise your awareness to it. You have already been doing this if you have tried any of the exercises offered earlier in this text. Now I am just calling a spade a spade so that we can take this discussion to a new level of understanding as we explore the higher vibrating aspect of ourselves.

With that said, individuals who foster a relationship with the superconscious have discovered several startling benefits. They tend to feel energized and experience more positive feelings about themselves and their lives. This connection reveals answers to life questions, including increased insights into their life path or purpose. Their ability to stay true to themselves, including the ability to say no, despite how others may feel, is augmented. These same individuals recount decreased negativity and an increased sense of self-love and gratitude.

They also find they can choose happiness daily and recognize that everything in life has a reason, including setbacks.

We can bypass dredging through our trauma by getting to know and accessing this little-discussed part of ourselves. We will not be looking into the dark, dank recesses of our minds to find answers, but instead will be looking up for our salvation. All it requires is our willingness to tap into this higher range of consciousness.

The Spirit In The Sky

The notion of a divine source is found in religions worldwide. The description tied to this unseen power varies from culture to culture, but the basic tenants held are consistent regardless of where you look. In the West, this supernatural force is commonly called 'God.' Around the world, this indescribable presence has been referred to as Yahweh, Allah, Brahma, Jehovah, Tiān, Shangdi, Viracocha, Anu, and Baiame. (I will be utilizing the term God in the male context, source, the universe, or the divine interchangeably to describe this higher power to ease and simplify our discussion.)

We really don't know much about God. Is God male or female, a supernatural being, a power, or a force underlying reality? Anything we might have to say is based upon faith and pure conjecture. God cannot be proven or disproven by the scientific method. It would be like trying to prove the existence of ultraviolet radiation. It, like God, is invisible and undetectable by the naked eye. We know of its existence because of its effect and the influence it has on the material world. We don't see the radiation, but we know we have been exposed to it when our skin gets burned on a hot sunny day.

The same holds true for God. God is not tangible, yet billions worldwide testify to their experiences with him and his substantial impact on their lives. They might not be able to see him, but they can feel his presence. God sits above our superconscious mind in the same way our superconscious sits above the subconscious. God, our superconscious, our conscious, and our subconscious mind work together, creating a unified system to facilitate the activities of our internal world.

Our superconscious mind, like our subconscious, is made up of several component parts, each of which function in different ways. Elements of the subconscious mind include our ego, our inner critic, our core beliefs, and our of preprogrammed scripts. The superconscious mind is made up of our soul, our higher self, and how energy or the divine moves through us. There are other structures and systems that comprise this unseen dimension, but the discussion of them is outside the scope of this work.

The Soul

Our vital soul, in a nutshell, houses our true selves. It is who we are. It exists throughout our being, throughout all of our levels of consciousness. Some associate the soul with our personality, where it represents the qualities we are born with unhindered by life experiences, family, societal programming, or trauma, all of which alter our perception of our inherent nature.

The soul is said to be immortal and transcends material existence. Anyone who believes in the afterlife believes in the existence of the soul. Our soul is a bridge between the divine and the physical world. When we become consciously aware of our soul, we become empowered to live the life we want. Living in alignment with our soul's desires offers us a more fulfilling, joyful, peaceful, and abundant life. Understanding the nature of our soul and how we interact with it helps set the stage for understanding our consciousness more meaningfully.

Some traditions divide the soul into two parts, our 'upper' or 'divine soul' and our 'lower' or 'animal soul.' Others describe the soul in terms of vibration or frequency. The higher the frequency, the closer to God. The lower the frequency, the further we are from this life-giving source. The upper or divine soul, the part of us that connects with God, vibrates at a higher frequency. Feelings of love, kindness, connectedness, charity, creativity, compassion, surrender, humility, and benevolence are tied to it. It supports our sense of self, our self-respect, and our integrity. It provides us with a sense of stability, especially during difficult times or when misfortune occurs.

The animal soul thrives on the satisfaction it receives from all things of the flesh. It is self-indulgent, selfish, arrogant, lustful, angry, prideful, and boastful. It perpetually seeks reward and pleasure while evading anything it might consider harmful to the self. People ruled by the lower soul do not rely on their integrity to make decisions. They are controlled by their hedonistic emotions upon which they will act and react. They do not reflect on situations but automatically respond to them based on their inner urges. I hope by now these attributes sound familiar. Yes, our ego is an aspect of the lower soul.

The upper and lower soul can be further broken down into a myriad of graduations, soul levels, or frequencies. Our soul level can change depending on where we are mentally or emotionally. We can, at times, find ourselves floundering in despair (lower soul), while at other times, we might feel blissful or in the midst of an ecstatic experience (upper soul). Our ability to gauge our soul level becomes more apparent, more perceptible, and increasingly obvious the more we quiet the mind, get into the present moment and look inside.

The Devolution Of The Soul

One of the best explanations I have found regarding gradations of the soul, from its connection to the divine to its lower levels of material existence, comes from Jewish mysticism. We are naturally connected to source when we emerge into this world. As we grow and are affected by life experiences, it shifts. The draw of the animal soul seduces us to turn our attention from the heart and focus on worldly matters. The more attention we place upon ourselves and our self-satisfaction, the more attached we become to these lower levels of consciousness. Today's world places a premium on this devolved aspect of our make-up.

The shifting of our energy does not happen all at once. It develops over time, instance by instance. We form what are described as peels, shells, or husks, 'kelipots' in Hebrew, that obscure our connection with the divine. These shells can be imagined as a series of concentric circles, like the layers of an onion, or even as Russian nesting dolls, the small wooden dolls of decreasing size that are placed one inside another. These obstructive layers interfere with our ability to access the upper soul. The more layers we have, the deeper we become entrenched in the dictates of the lower soul. We become increasingly blind to the guidance our divine soul has to offer.

These shells leave us feeling separate, disconnected from source and the life-giving energy it provides. The more shrouded the soul becomes, the more it looks to the world for sustenance. Some people's divine souls are so overwhelmed by the calling of their animal souls it causes them to rely on other people and situations as a substitute for the revitalizing vigor God provides.

For example, a person with narcissistic traits is heavily influenced by layer upon layer of shells. They take what they want from others to get the nourishment needed to fill their inner void. Sadly, it is never enough. They keep taking and taking so they can feel whole and satisfied. Sadly, the physical world does not provide the soul with the nourishment it needs to survive. This can only be accomplished by cultivating a connection with God via the superconscious mind.

The Battle For Your Soul

Strange as this may sound, a battle is going on inside you, waging a war for your mind. The fight is between your divine and animal souls, your ego and your true self, good and evil, or God and the Devil himself. The objective? Control over you! The upper and lower souls are both vying for your attention. Which side you choose to follow is totally up to you.

The divine soul does not force you to follow it. It might remind you and even nag you to pay attention, but it doesn't use clandestine ploys to exhort control. It leaves it up to you. You can follow its suggestions or not. On the other hand, when the animal soul discovers itself in a diminished position, it will attempt to push its way back into your life. It will create issues for you to contend with to distract your concentration from the feel-good feelings the upper soul provides. It will employ anxiety, fear, negative thoughts, and your inner critic to lure you back. It wants to keep you held hostage to your own negative thinking.

Don't let the lower soul fool you. By now, you are already becoming aware of when these kinds of thoughts and emotions arise. Know they are coming from your animal soul, and rejoice.

Laugh at your lower soul. You have caught it in one of its nefarious ploys attempting to lead you astray.

Exercise:

You can use times when the animal soul attempts to get you into its clutches by reflecting on the situation. Ask questions such as *"What was it trying to lure me with?"* or *"What temptations did it use in an attempt to ensnare me back down to my lower self?"* I think by now you have come to understand that when we are in bed with our ego and animal soul, we feel bad inside. Spotting this lesser aspect of yourself with its fingers in the cookie jar might be enough for you to not be swayed.

Our Higher Self

Our higher self is an aspect of the divine soul. We use it to interact with the superconscious mind. On some levels, our higher self can be thought of as the voice of the soul, just like our inner critic is the voice of the ego. Many believe our higher self fills our lives with purpose and meaning. It opens us up to moments of inspiration and guides us to the truth of our essence. This connection helps us stay centered in moments of adversity and supports us in the direction our lives take.

Our soul knows what we need in every moment. Our higher self is tasked with leading us in that direction. Our higher self constantly reminds us of what we should be doing or where we should be heading. It also advises us on precautions we should be taking. Our soul and higher self always have our best interests in mind.

Our higher self is always available to us and loves it when we ask it questions. For example, when individuals contemplate actions to take during a tricky situation and ask, *"What should I do now?"* or *"What Would Jesus Do?"* this conscious act of introspection automatically connects them with the guidance the higher self offers. An answer is always provided. We can choose to listen to the advice we receive, or we can reject it, resist it, ignore it, or run away from it. You have already begun developing a relationship with your higher self when you explored the reflection questions earlier. You asked your higher self for insights, and it gratefully provided them to you.

This voice can be drowned out by the influence the ego and lower soul has over us. Although not intentional, we often allow our logical mind, our fears, worries, ideas, judgments, past experiences, and preconceived notions to get in the way. This causes us to lose touch with our higher self, vital soul, and ultimately God.

Our relationship with our higher self doesn't happen instantly or automatically. We have to want it. It needs to be cultivated, nurtured, and developed. We have to heed its presence in our lives. Communicating with the higher self is the practice of surrendering to our higher purpose. Some will say we must be willing to be 'led by spirit' and allow God to lead. The freer we become of material attachments and the pressing demands of the lower soul, the easier it is to recognize the communication our higher self offers.

What It Feels Like To Receive A Message

Our higher self is always talking to us. We receive messages daily. The question is: are you listening? We often blow off its commentary as unimportant, inconsequential, or relegate it to the working of a stray or imaginary thought. When we do not follow the insights received, we end up paying the consequence. Then we wonder why we didn't listen to ourselves in the first place.

You think about bringing a sweater to work but don't and end up freezing in a meeting. The thought of taking an alternative route to the store crosses your mind for some reason. You don't pay attention and find yourself stuck in bumper-to-bumper traffic. You inexplicably dread attending an upcoming social engagement but go anyway, only to run into your ex. Yikes!

The voice of your higher self never talks to you like your inner critic. It often comes forward as a seemingly casual comment, a single word, or a short phrase. It is never mean or nasty and will never leave you feeling anxious or worried. It won't judge or criticize you and it never tries to occupy your attention or focus. Even if a message reveals a difficult truth you have been avoiding, its communication is always shrouded in patience and love. It does not come to hurt you. It offers its guidance as a means to help you grow. You will surprisingly find yourself filled with a strong, clear sense of determination and purpose once you accept and surrender to its promptings.

It is not only through the small, still voice we have inside that we can communicate and align with this higher power. You may obtain insights from strange and unlikely sources. You may have a sudden urge to do something. An image could appear in your mind's eye. You may have a dream about a situation. The answer to your question might be found in the book you are reading, on the radio, or coming out of the mouth of others. Strange as it is to say, it is possible to differentiate God's words coming to us via the higher self from the egoic commentary of the animal soul.

You may doubt what I am saying about the higher self now. You can always write the experience off as some weird synchronicity or uncanny coincidence. But it is not. I challenge you. Use your own life to see if what I am claiming is true. Look for the evidence. You can check the veracity of this concept by tracking the transmissions you get throughout the day. It doesn't matter if you act on the insights you receive or not. What is more important is to admit you did, receive the communication.

Over time, I hope you will discover that your higher self's guidance is accurate, and you will begin to trust the messages you encounter. Surprisingly, the frequency you receive these insights will increase the more you put this practice into play. This is because you are creating a stronger connection with your higher self. It is like building a new neural pathway in the brain, except this one is with God.

Inspired Action

There is a second part to working with your higher self that should seem obvious, but I will say it out loud anyway. Our actions are the bridge between our thoughts and reality. These communications, once received, do require we do something. It is not the knee-jerk reaction we encounter when discussing the subconscious mind but inspired action. Divinely inspired action always comes from the heart and not the head.

I can't say this enough, don't be fooled by mistaking promptings of the ego for messages from your higher self. These lower soul communications, disguised as a directive from God, were my downfall. We feel energized, enthusiastic, happy, or joyful when we take inspired actions. Actions prompted by the lower self usually leave us feeling stressed, anxious, or fatigued. We are not excited, enthusiastic, uplifted, or motivated to move forward. Often it feels like a struggle.

The ego says, *"Run, run, run!" "Hurry, hurry, hurry!" "Oh no, the world is coming to an end!"* This is not God talking to you but your preprogrammed scripts playing out in the background. Slow down. Become mindful if you are unsure where the message is coming from. Reflect on it. Journal about it. And most importantly, breathe. You've got this.

I have so many stories I could share about taking inspired action, with just as many which talk about how the universe was screaming at me, and I didn't listen. Here are a couple of trivial, humdrum encounters in which I actually took notice. It is not the grandiosity of the situations. The glory is in the details.

My dishwasher went on the fritz during the Christmas holiday. I called my service guy, but he was going to be out of town until after the New Year. The bottom of the dishwasher was full of water. Would the small ocean of murky liquid start to smell? I didn't want to find out. So there I am, sitting on the floor with a small cup, a bucket, and a handful of ShamWow towels at the ready.

It seemed apparent from the get-go this method was less than stellar. So I asked myself, *"What can I use to make this go faster?"* Immediately I see the turkey baster in my mind's eyes. Yes, you heard me right, the turkey baster. You don't know how happy I was to get an answer. Granted, it took a while to drain almost 4 gallons of liquid from the bottom of my dishwasher, but it went faster and smoother than my earlier idea. Thank God!

Here is another quick yet mundane example of receiving messages from our higher self and the rewards of taking inspired action.

I was visiting my friend Cyndie for the weekend. As I brushed my teeth, I noticed the bathroom sink was not draining correctly. Apparently, the upstairs air conditioner drains through the bathroom sink's plumbing. It had backed up once before, causing significant damage. Cyndie was stressed, and when she tried to reach her plumber, his phone went straight to voicemail. This only added to her anxiety.

Well, they say, God moves in mysterious ways... Fast forward to later in the day. I was out running errands and got into my car to head back to Cyndie's house. I like listening to talk radio, and as I started my car, a home improvement show was airing. Imagine my surprise when the topic of conversation revolved around how an air conditioner can cause sinks to stop up because of fungal growth in the drain line.

I could feel spirit buzzing through me as I made my way down the road. I knew that what they recommended would do the trick because I have learned to trust and acknowledge the messages I receive. They suggested pouring bleach or vinegar down the drain to unclog it. When I returned to Cyndie's, we did what the guy on the radio recommended, and Bam! The drain was unplugged, just like he described. We were both thanking God for that one.

Our Indelible Spirit

In the Bible, the word 'spirit' most often refers to 'God's power in action.' This unseen, elusive, active force, 'the breath of life,' was imbued into man, animating him. This unknowable, life force energy sustains all created things. It is the power that activates us and infuses everyone and everything with life.

The concept of an intangible, spiritual energy was well understood by our ancestors. They all seem to agree on one thing regardless of where you look. This animating life force is what governs our existence. It enters the body at conception and leaves us when we die. It is known as 'neshamah' in Hebrew. In Christianity, it is referred to as the 'Holy Spirit.' The Greeks called it 'pneuma.' In Africa, it is identified as 'ashe,' while in Hawaii, it is called 'mana.' It is called qi, chi, prana, or shakti in the East. It has also been described as orgone, psionic energy, scalar waves, biofield, and life force energy.

This concept of chi, or our life force energy, is a well-developed concept in Eastern traditions. It is believed that spirit descends from higher levels of existence and moves into the body through the top of our head. It then travels through channels down our backs until it reaches our feet and the denseness of the earth, only to return through the body to source.

Eastern traditions contend that health is experienced when our 'chi' moves unencumbered. Mental, emotional, spiritual, and physical issues will present themselves when resistance is encountered. Thus, radiant health, and enlightenment, can be achieved by reducing or eliminating blockages to the flow of this life-giving force.

A similar idea is explored in Kabbalistic texts. Spirit, in this ancient Jewish tradition, moves through a series of 'sefirot' (spheres) and paths which represent the conduit this animating force travels through the mental, emotional, and the physical aspects of the self. I could write an entire book dedicated to the implications of the movement of spirit through the body. Oh wait, I already did! It is called *Avoiding The Cosmic 2 x 4*.

Spirit can also be viewed from a more modern perspective. Some liken our life force energy to the flow of electricity through a conductor like a wire. You plug a light into an outlet (source), and the light turns on (us). A more accurate way of portraying how spirit moves through our bodies is by having the same light but by adding a dimmer switch to the circuit. A dimmer switch varies the electrical current going to the bulb, thus controlling its illumination level. The light shines bright when the flow of electricity through the circuit is uninhibited. It begins to dim when resistance is added. The more resistance, the dimmer the bulb.

Regardless of what it is called when your spirit aligns with your higher self, your soul, and with God, your inner vibration rises, and your negative thoughts and emotions fade. The real you, unencumbered by life programming, can step forward. You are tapped in, tuned in, and turned on when you align yourself with source. Any knots or bends in your electrical wires straighten out in this state, and spirit can move through you without resistance. Your inner light can shine brightly.

I like calling this state of alignment 'being in the flow.' Athletes commonly refer to it as 'being in the zone.' 'Getting your groove on,' or 'being filled with the Holy Spirit' are other ways this surge of vitalizing force is described.

Going With The Flow

We have all had moments of being in the flow. We are in the flow when we are absorbed in an activity. Time seems to slip away, and what we are doing happens effortlessly. Our worries, fears, resistance, anxiety, and boredom, as well as our stress hormones, disappear and are replaced by high-energy, positive emotions. There is an absence of inner chatter. The mind slows down, and a sense of calmness preails.

Think of the musician who is absorbed in their performance. These individuals are in a flow state. They are open and allow spirit to naturally and freely move through them. The same holds true for the scientist, the engineer, the mathematician, the teacher, and even the housewife. They may spend countless hours struggling to find the solution to a problem. Finally, in a state of rest, when their conscious mind is taken off of their dilemma, the answer magically appears. This is also an indication of being in alignment with source and in the flow. Our resistance is low, allowing our life force energy to move freely. Our connection to the divine is re-established. The answers, once hidden, are revealed.

Nevertheless, the vast majority of us have resistance on our electrical lines. This resistance comes from our life experiences, our traumas, our egos, our negative thinking, and our preprogrammed responses. It reflects the many layers of shells within our souls, which are there every hour of every day until we do something about it.

The movement of spirit shuts down even further when we are upset. The worse you feel, the worse it gets. Said in another way, when we feel good, have positive emotions, and are calm and grounded, the resistance we experience is reduced. We are open and flowing.

Being in a deleterious state, when we have bad mojo going on, are in a bad mood, are angry, frustrated, anxious, annoyed, or trapped in our rabbit hole, turns down this energy current. How we feel in our inner world is directly related to the activity of this vitalizing force. This is why sometimes we can feel so connected to source and at other times, well, not so much.

The best way to enter back into the stream of spirit is to balance and center our inner world. You know the drill. Take a break from what you are doing and contemplate silently or select something that brings you joy or makes you feel good. Employ one of the many mindfulness techniques we have already discussed, which will naturally relax the body and quiet the mind putting you back into the flow.

What you do really doesn't matter. Read spiritual or uplifting materials, sing, dance, pray, or chant. Meditation, yoga, tai chi, or an intense workout at the gym can get your energy moving again. So can hiking, fishing, or working on a creative project. You can also get into the flow while raking leaves, weeding the garden, mowing the lawn, sweeping the floor, or cleaning a bathroom. What is required is your focus. Any activity done mindfully supports the movement of spirit.

And don't bother trying to force yourself back into the flow with sheer determination. This only increases your inner resistance. Sometimes we have to ride it out. Do things to nurture yourself if you find yourself in this situation, and love yourself even more if things seem really chaotic.

You can also ask your higher self for guidance by asking questions such as *"What should I be doing right now?"* It will be happy to provide you with an answer. Be open to receiving its reply. What it suggests is ever changing. What you need today may not be what your soul needs tomorrow. And you never know. You might be guided to go scrub your kitchen floors. You may be laughing at me right now, but I am willing to bet you will experience a sense of calm, grounded satisfaction if the task is divinely inspired.

Final Thoughts

You might wonder why I am bringing up all this talk of God and spirit and your higher self. You might also be curious what this has to do with transforming your inner world. Weird as it is to say, it has everything to do with it. When we consciously shift our focus and become increasingly aware of our inner world, we automatically begin connecting with higher levels of consciousness. This frees up our energy, increases our vibration, and allows spirit to move unimpeded through us. It acts as a catalyst to transcend the many shells interfering with our happiness and feelings of contentment. It supports us as we break free from the clutches of our inner judge, our inner critic, the ego and the animal soul.

This connection opens us up to our most enlightened self, where we can tap into its wisdom and connect authentically with God. Some people call this highly energized state 'Christ Consciousness', 'Samadhi', and even the 'Kingdom of Heaven' within.

We are the arbiter of our fate. We have the power to choose. We can choose to stop, contemplate and connect with our higher selves, or we can allow our preprogrammed responses to rule. When we surrender to the prompting we receive, we can let go and let God navigate our lives, resistance-free. By doing this, we can emerge victorious in our battle over the self, and a whole new world can emerge.

Oh No! Not Positive Emotions!

"Your feelings aren't random, they are messengers. And if you want to get anywhere, you need to be able to let them speak to you, and tell you want you really need."
— Brianna Wiest

We have discussed negative, lower-vibrating emotions ad nauseam, so now, we are going to start moving up the emotional ladder to something bigger and better. The reality is; there are only two states of being. In one state, we experience joy, happiness, and harmony. We are in alignment with God, source, and the universe. This allows spirit to flow freely through us, leaving us feeling optimistic, upbeat, and connected. The other is one filled with stress and chaos. We are out of alignment and out of the flow. Our energy channels are constricted, and the movement of our life force energy is reduced, causing us to feel down, stuck and disconnected.

We can choose which state we want to live in. We choose to be in the flow and allied with source and our divine soul, or we can choose to be out of the flow and contend with our egos and all that it implies. When we focus our attention on positive, uplifting thoughts about ourselves and our life experiences, we move back into the flow. We move out of alignment when we constantly fixate on how messed up we are or how life never gives us a break.

Very little is written regarding the brighter side of our emotional being. It is as if being happy or having a positive outlook on life is some deep dark clandestine topic we are not supposed to talk about, much less explore. More importantly, many of us do not know what happiness feels like. (In this context, I am using the word happy to refer to experiencing any positive emotions.) We might correlate our sense of happiness with "*my life doesn't suck right now*" or those brief moments of calm waters before the impending storm.

I know I have had moments of feeling good inside, of being happy, but those times were always short-lived and fleeting. It seemed as if my euphoric world would quickly come crashing down around me, the exuberant thrill being viciously taken away. It is interesting because I can readily dredge up innumerable hard luck stories, complete with the intricate, salient details surrounding my hurt, pain, and trauma. When I look to recount my countless blessings, in many cases, the best I can offer is *"It was good."*

A part of me questioned whether this state actually existed or if the whole concept of happiness was just one big concocted fantasy. However, some people can obtain this desirable state. They were the lucky ones, the happy ones, the ones whose lives always seemed to work. I despised them (just kidding), but I did long to have what seemed so elusive to me. Being happy on a regular basis was right up there with believing I could marry the 'formal dance' date from the *Mystery Date Game*. I didn't think it was possible.

In the truest sense of the word, happiness is identified as a transient experience. We feel happy based on external events, often tied to an experience, an idea, or a destination. We get a new job. We are engaging in a fun activity. Finding a twenty dollar bill in our pocket might make us happy or talking with an old friend. Watching it rain outside or seeing a beautiful sunset might bring up this emotion. Climbing into bed after changing the sheets or taking a hot bath can help fill our happiness quota.

These situations make us smile, at least in the moment, but they do not change our 'emotional set point.' Our emotional set point is where we automatically go when a core belief is aroused. Suppose our emotional set point regarding money is to experience worry, fear, or destitution when we have to spend some. In that case, our emotions will immediately shift to this most practiced, predominant, automatic response.

This may make us think happiness is a hit-or-miss experience, but here is the truth regarding happiness. Being happy is not a permanent state. It is a goal. Let me say that again. Being happy is not a permanent state. It is a goal. Happiness is something we cultivate in our inner world. It all comes down to where we focus our attention. We can choose to interact with life from our well-trained, downbeat emotional state, or we can focus on what makes us feel good.

As we look to recalibrate our inner equilibrium, an excellent place to start is to define a number of elusive and heartfelt feelings. We use words such as happiness, contentment, hopefulness, optimism, enthusiasm, passion, and joy, but what are they really? Defining these terms may help us recognize them when they appear in our lives. It is impossible to strive for something, much less know if we are in the midst of it if we don't know what to look for. You might have experienced one or two upbeat feelings without ever realizing it.

Ester Hicks, in her book *Ask and It is Given*, offers a road map to our emotions. She identifies fear and powerlessness at the bottom of the scale and joy at the upper end of the emotional spectrum. Hicks considers boredom, the blasé feeling we may have, as a neutral spot in our psyche. When we are bored, we are not happy, but at the same time, we are not sad, angry, lonely, or afraid. We are simply bored. The emotions below boredom are heavier, more painful, and progressively destructive, while the emotions listed above boredom become increasingly positive, lighter, and of a higher vibration.

Moving Up The Scale Of Positive Emotions

Hierarchy Of Emotions

Level	Emotion
1	Joy
2	Passion
3	Enthusiasm
4	Positive Beliefs

Hierarchy Of Emotions
Continued

5	Optimism
6	Hopefulness
7	Contentment
8	Boredom
9	Pessimism
10	Frustration/Irritation
11	Overwhelmed
12	Disappointment
13	Doubt
14	Worry
15	Blame
16	Discouragement
17	Anger
18	Revenge
19	Hatred/Rage
20	Jealousy
21	Insecurity/Guilt/Unworthiness
22	Fear/Powerlessness
23	Rabbit Hole (My addition)

Contentment

We arrive at contentment when we move up the emotion scale from boredom. Contentment refers to a state of feeling satisfied.

Things are okay, maybe not great, but we have nothing to complain about. When one reaches this level, there is a sense of calmness and inner stability. Our negative thinking is reduced.

Contentment comes from realizing we can be happy with what we already have. When we are content, we are pleased with our lives and can experience a tentative state of inner peace. There is a level of acceptance that allows us to step back and enjoy the beauty of living.

Hopefulness

Hopefulness encompasses a mindset where we can see the brighter side of things. It is the driving force that sits behind every one of our endeavors. It is like contentment, only better! It uses inspiration and the chance of favorable outcomes to spur on the achievement of our desires.

You don't just sit around and wait for things to miraculously happen. Hopefulness allows us to set goals and causes us to look for possibilities when none seem readily apparent. It promotes an attitude of growth and success. Hope is also something we can hold on to when life throws us a curveball. It keeps us company in our darkest hours and gives us the courage to keep going.

Optimism

Optimism is an attitude characterized by a belief that the outcome of an endeavor will be positive. It takes hope and imbues it with confidence and strength. You don't just hope for a good result; you expect it.

People who are optimistic see the brighter side of things. They believe in themselves and their abilities. They will continue working towards their goals even in the face of hardships. They view obstacles as temporary setbacks or as learning experiences. Optimistic people believe that even after a bad day, tomorrow will be better. This provides them the strength and fortitude to keep moving forward.

Positive Beliefs

We have already discussed the general nature of core beliefs. Our negative core beliefs can include: *"I'm dumb," "I'm fat," "I'm invisible"* or *"I don't matter,"* These pessimistic views of ourselves activate our internal scripts and typically come to the surface via our inner critic. But not everything in our inner world is negative.

On the other end of the spectrum, positive beliefs can include, *"Life is good," "I'm confident," "People like me," "I can do this,"* and *"I will overcome."* Positive beliefs build us up. They reflect confidence in who we are and what we do. Our attitude is no longer just a hope for a desired outcome. It is ingrained into the very fiber of our being. Anyone who would try to dissuade us would be challenged. Believe it or not, we all have positive beliefs about ourselves.

Enthusiasm

There is an unspoken energy, an excitement, which exists behind enthusiasm. Enthusiasm causes us to have a zest for life. It is the fire we feel inside that drives us forward to do something we love. Enthusiasm causes us to do things, not just because it is required but because of a deep desire to achieve it. We do it because we want to.

People who are enthusiastic exhibit a playful joy in their endeavors. They are full of energy and are willing to take risks. They have the courage, confidence, and creativity tied to a willingness to engage in new projects or ideas. They are eager to give their time and energy to attain their goals. They have unwavering faith in themselves and believe any roadblocks they encounter can be overcome.

Passion

Passionate people have an underlying drive that keeps them going regardless of the hurdles they may encounter. They are on a 'mission from God' doing their life's work and will stick to their vision come hell or high water. They love what they do, and to many, the money doesn't matter. Work does not feel like work to these individuals. They feel fulfilled in the accomplishment. Even if a task does not excite them, they will complete it to realize their aspirations.

Some people view the passionate person as being obsessed, but their life is their purpose, and their purpose is their life. They are willing to humble themselves to a task and accept sacrifices to achieve their goals. When you live a life filled with passion, you are aligned with who you really are inside. You are aligned with your core beliefs and values.

Joy

There is an intense, consuming feeling of positivity when we experience joy. All negative emotions disappear. We are happy, content, enthusiastic, inspired, and filled with creativity. There is an overwhelming feeling of hopefulness. In moments of joy, our face may light up. We might find ourselves involuntarily grinning from ear to ear. We might have a sparkle in our eyes, or at times, we may even seem to be glowing. We might feel excited or euphoric. We might begin laughing, singing, or dancing.

There is a presence of love for ourselves and others when we experience joy. Joyful people recognize that difficult circumstances do arise and feelings such as sadness and loneliness are a normal part of living. They do not let these negative feelings get them down for long. They can find the silver lining even in the toughest of times.

Some authors suggest that when we experience joy, there is an 'exultation of soul,' where we rejoice in rapturous delight at having reached the highest level of salvation. When we are in the throes of joy, we have confidence that all of our needs will be provided for. We feel connected, content, and one with the universe.

Did you notice as we moved further up the ladder, there was increased clarity of who we are and what we want? You might also have noticed that the higher we climbed, our confidence and determination increased? With each step up, our emotions are moving into higher realms, higher vibrations, and with it, a closer connection to God.

Roadmap To Our Emotions

How we feel inside can be used to navigate our everyday lives. When our thoughts are focused on what we want, what we are passionate about, when we feel a deep-seated impulse to move forward, an unexplained eagerness towards something, AND we are in alignment with source, we feel magnificent. When our thoughts focus on what we don't have and don't want, we feel awful. It is akin to the difference between attending a live concert where one of our favorite bands is playing versus doing our taxes. We feel the thrill and excitement of one and the dread and agony of the other. One is effortless, the other... torture.

I like to think of my emotions as messages from my soul. They let me know how I feel at any given moment. I use them like a traffic light. Healthy, pleasant, and uplifting emotions indicate it is safe to proceed. I am heading in the right direction, am acting in my best interests, and am serving my higher purpose.

Alarm bells going off inside tells me I should take caution and beware. I am being alerted to the fact that my thinking is leading me off the path of joy, especially when I find myself in the heat of anger, frustration, sadness, guilt, or grief-stricken. I use this warning signal as an opportunity to take a step back and evaluate what is going on.

Some people use their emotions as a barometer to analyze the current state of their internal affairs. Their emotions help them identify where they are on a soul level. They use them to gauge whether they are in alignment with the universe, in a flow state, or if their life force energy has slowed down. Negative emotions, in particular, offer them clues into areas needing healing. When triggered, they use them to communicate with their higher self and ask why the emotion surfaced.

When we live our lives guided by our emotional state, we cannot help but live in soul's purpose. We can use them to feel our way back into vibrational alignment. Consciously adjusting to what is happening inside will keep our frequency high and out of the clutches of our ego and inner critic. The measure is not *"How do I feel today?"* but *"How am I feeling right now?"* You might have felt great five minutes ago, but then you received a phone call from your boss that sent all those good feelings right out the window.

Feeling The Shift

A simple fact of life is that no one has positive emotions all of the time. Life also doesn't mean we will stop encountering challenges or have times when we are unhappy, frustrated, lonely, or sad. We can use these setbacks to dig a little deeper into ourselves and grow. The key to long-lasting happiness is about raising our awareness to the moment our emotions start heading in a downward direction. This shift is a clue our thoughts have gone awry, and we are moving out of alignment.

You might be detecting a drop in your energy when your breathing shallows; you feel pain in your stomach, or heaviness in your chest. Finding fault in yourself or others, being cranky, complaining, or having your inner critic in full swing can also signal that your energy has shifted. Feeling anxious, doubtful, fearful, or just bad would also be a good indication to take a slight mindfulness pause and check inside to recalibrate your thinking.

All you need is one idea, one new thought to change how you are feeling inside. It doesn't have to be about the matter at hand. It can be about anything, anything that will move your focus from the low-vibrating thought you are having to something healthier. If your new thought choice makes you feel bad, pick something else. The goal is to find something that feels better.

Trying to analyze what is going on keeps the negativity alive. Beating yourself up for what you are experiencing exacerbates the situation and makes matters worse. Think about it. Your negative thoughts aren't going away or changing into something else while you are paying attention to them. This only increases their momentum, taking you further away from source and increasingly out of the flow.

When you let them go, they will stop. Surrendering to the situation and accepting it for what it is helps you to move on. Surrender opens the door for the emergence of hope and optimism. You might not know what will happen or why something is manifesting in your life, but when we encounter higher emotions, a part of us always knows things will improve.

When you detect a downward swing, 17-second rule it. Breathing, tapping, or working with any of the mindfulness exercises we have discussed earlier can do the trick. So can taking a moment to appreciate someone or something. Think of the good thing going on in your life and say, *"Thank you."* Moments of gratitude will always silence the worry, fear, or doubt within you and bring you closer to God.

Sometimes, when trying to find our bliss, a higher vibrating emotional state may seem miles away. Maybe you are hanging out in your rabbit hole. Perhaps your inner critic is running on overdrive. You might be telling yourself some very colorful, abet negative tales. The objective is not about having a perfect new thought. It is about having a better feeling one. It is impossible to jump from a low vibrating thought to one that is all sparkly, yet even a slightly higher one can offer you some relief. It may not be the highest or most positive thought you could have, but it is probably better than where you are at the moment.

Final Thoughts

Don't get discouraged if you cannot shift your emotional space from the depths of despair to feeling like you are on top of the world in one fell swoop. Our emotions shift in increments. Anger feels better than depression. While it is not bliss, you still might feel a bit better. At least your inner state is moving in the right direction, up the emotional ladder.

Give yourself a moment to hold onto this new vibration. You might find another higher, more positive one entering your awareness that you can grab hold of. Be with this one as well. In no time at all, with a small effort on your part, you will begin significantly shifting your inner experience.

The Game Of Life And How To Play It

*"Watch your thoughts, they become your words;
Watch your words, they become your actions;
Watch your actions, they become your habits;
Watch your habits, they become your character;
Watch your character, it becomes your destiny."*

- Lao Tzu

I have laid some heavy concepts on you that I hope you will take into consideration. You may have begun looking at how some of them are already playing out in your life. Fantastic as some of this material may sound to you, we are going to take it even further, raising your awareness to another aspect of our being directly connected with the activities of our inner world. Would you believe that each of us, yes, you, me, all of your friends, and all of your family members transmit 'energy,' their personal vibration, out into the world? Would you also believe you can also receive the broadcast others project!

I know, shocking, isn't it? Yet built into each of us are the capabilities to publicize the undisclosed truth of who we are, just like a radio station transmits music out into the either. Also, part and parcel of who we are includes the mechanisms necessary to receive transmissions, not only from God but from everyone else on the planet.

Picture this... You are driving down the road and glance at the person in the next car rocking out to a song. Out of curiosity, you find yourself gazing at their enthusiastic, abet funny behavior. The next thing you know, the person behind the wheel abruptly stops jamming and looks over at you. You might think to yourself, *"Busted,"* but what happened? You were projecting your attention out into the world, which the other driver detected and reacted to.

This also happens in reverse. Think of times when you have been behind the wheel and got a strange urge to look into the car next to you. Your quick glance reveals a little girl sitting in the back seat, staring at you with a sweet smile on her face. She was broadcasting her energy; you received it and acted on it. Aka, you looked.

We constantly radiate the vibration of our unique emotional landscape out into the environment. This signal emanates from us like ripples form in the water when a stone is tossed in. We transmit what is happening inside us day by day and moment by moment. It is out there in plain sight, available for everyone to see. It doesn't matter if you try to put on a happy face or attempt to mask your dastardly intentions. What you are projecting is your current mental and emotional state, regardless of how much you may try to conceal it.

People sense your 'vibes' even if they don't recognize it as a communication from this unseen dimension. You do not have to be particularly sensitive to discern someone who has 'good energy' from someone who doesn't. We often steer clear of individuals who feel mean or angry with no objective evidence. Their hostility might be so intense we can feel it from all the way across the room. We might also have a strange attraction to people who impart feelings of love, caring, or empathy. We might not know or understand why we are drawn to them. We just are.

We tend to receive transmissions from the people we love, our close friends and family members, the easiest. We might think they can read our minds, but they are actually just picking up what we are inadvertently expressing. Our awareness of their broadcasts often diminishes as we get to know someone. It is not that they aren't sending out a glaring signal. Instead, we have become accustomed to the vibration they give off.

So, why am I bringing up this topic in the first place? Great question! Our focus is not on the reception of these signals but, more importantly, on what we are broadcasting. Every emotion we experience radiates a signal. When we have powerful emotions, it is as if we have turned up the volume, sending a louder, stronger message out into the world.

The emotions we experience, moreover, reflect the tone of our transmission. Each emotion we feel vibrates at a specific frequency. In his book *Power vs. Force*, Dr. David Hawkins created a 'map of consciousness' depicting the vibration and tone of the emotions we emit. The frequencies are measured in Hertz. One Hertz (Hz) implies one vibration per second, while 60 Hz indicates 60 vibrations per second. The greater the Hertz, the more connected we feel to God or source.

Our personal vibration changes throughout the day. It all depends on what is going on inside. We might vibrate at the level of 'love' (500 Hz) when petting our dog or going for a walk in the park. We might vibrate at the level of 'fear' (100 Hz) when we think about money. Again, it is all about our thoughts and the emotional response we have to what we are thinking about.

Map Of Consciousness

Emotion	Hertz Level
Enlightenment	700-100
Peace	600
Joy	540
Love	500
Reason	400
Acceptance	350
Willingness	30
Neutrality	250
Courage	200
Pride	175
Anger	150
Desire	125
Fear	100
Greif	75
Apathy	50
Guilt	30
Shame	0 - 20

Our life experiences, our choices, decisions, our moments of glory, or our perceived failure, create the content of our inner world and our unique broadcast. Imagine how embarrassing it would be if scientists figured out how to harness our personal transmission and air it for everyone to see. What would they be watching? A Hallmark movie, or would it be more like a horror thriller?

Everyone's vibration is different. What we project is as unique as a fingerprint. We have our habitual state, the place we are most of the time, and then there is the place we go when an emotion is stimulated.

Even a slight shift in our emotional state changes the narrative of our emissions. People who are traditionally happy and joyful or find themselves easily appreciating someone or something, this is what they project. The happier they are, the higher their emitted vibration becomes.

People who walk around feeling ashamed, embarrassed, saying negative things to themselves, are angry, frustrated, impatient, cranky, or depressed, their vibration is lower and denser. This is also announced to the world. The lower they go, so does their emission.

When we make a fundamental change to our inner being, rewriting our old core beliefs, and modifying our negative thoughts, our personal vibration changes from a low-density one to something higher, lighter, and freer.

Exercise

Take a moment to stop and ponder, *"What am I projecting out into the universe?"* What thoughts are occupying your mind?

What emotional responses are they creating? Are your thoughts happy, helping to move you up to a higher soul level, or are they fear-based and ego-driven, which will take you down a notch or two or five?

The Law Of Attraction

We are going to take a slight detour, a tangent from our current conversation, and spend a bit of time talking about a very New Age concept called the 'Law of Attraction.' You may have already heard of it, and that is great. If this is new to you, let me lay down a bit of foundation.

In a nutshell, proponents of the Law of Attraction suggest we create our reality. They claim 'like attracts like.' They indicate what we focus on or habitually think about will be drawn into our personal experience. If there is something we want, all we need to do is focus on it, and it will miraculously come to us. Positive thoughts attract positive results, while negative ones attract discord and less-than-desirable outcomes.

The roots of the Law of Attraction go back to deep antiquity, with its tenants found in indigenous cultures, Christian writing, and many Eastern traditions. These philosophical systems focus on quieting the mind and looking inward to align ourselves with source. This notion can be seen in quotes such as: *"The universe is change; our life is what our thoughts make it."* – Marcus Aurelius Antoninus. *"All that we are is the result of what we have thought."* – Buddha. *"Do not conform to the pattern of this world, but be transformed, by the renewing of your mind."* – Romans 12:2.

A more systematic exploration of this theory dates back to the early 19th century with authors such as Helena Blavatsky, Thomas Troward, and William Walker Atkinson and the advent of the 'New Thought' movement. These early spiritual writers emphasized how our opinion of ourselves shapes our identities. When we change our inner perception, we can create a better, happier life beyond the constraints of our toxic programming. The material they offer is presented with a more modern, scientific flair.

Then, for some reason, things changed. The focus of this concept shifted from getting to know ourselves, looking inward to transform our thinking and our approach to life, to taking on a much more materialistic stance. Books like Wallace Delois Wattles', *The Science of Getting Rich* and Napoleon Hill's *Think And Grow Rich* were released. The techniques and methods they describe are consistent with the earlier writers, but the overall objective moved from finding happiness, contentment, and inner peace to manifesting material gains.

A resurgence of interest in the Law of Attraction occurred after the release of Rhonda Bryne's book and subsequent film *The Secret* in 2006. The Law of Attraction entered mainstream awareness. Many modern advocates began suggesting: if you think about something intense enough, if you pray for it vigorously, if you make a vision board, or repeat affirmations relentlessly, it will be yours. Their teachings leave the student believing all they need to do is ask, and their desires will manifest out of thin air.

This mindset made working with the Law of Attraction sound easy and straightforward. You think about something, and BAM, it happens. Sweet! The specific advice traditionally offered to bring your dreams into reality include: visualizing what you want, reframing your mindset from one of scarcity and lack to abundance, telling the universe precisely what you want, speaking it into existence, finding gratitude in all you do, and looking for synchronicities as an indicator you are on the right track.

True, true, and true. These pieces must be in place for the Law of Attraction to work. What is often ignored in this simplistic approach is the real work involved in modifying our inner world. It requires a careful combination of an awareness of our thoughts and emotions, being open to our soul's guidance, and taking inspired action.

I'll bet by now you can see why I am delving into this concept. In one form or another, I have offered many specific insights regarding how to shift your internal mindset and align with source. You may have already started to apply some of its precepts in your life.

My goal, and the goal of this book, has always been focused on helping you to move from suffering to contentment. There is a reason why I am including this section at all. It is because if the work we are doing to heal our inner world happens to bring us a new car, our soul mate, or millions of dollars, I'm all in.

Nevertheless, I have concerns regarding how the modern tenants of the Law of Attraction are being disseminated. As we have already discussed, making money and having 'things' comes from the ego and the lower soul. Our attention should always be pointed inward and upward on our thoughts, feelings, and our alignment. When we entertain the idea of doing something with the sole intent of making money or being successful, our focus is not on ourselves and our connection to God but on what we can get. As they say, the devil is in the details.

The Fine Print

Many of us spend all our time thinking about what we don't want and not nearly enough time on what we do. We ask for success but steadily believe we are going to fail. Even when we think about abundance and prosperity, a new love in our life, or whatever we truly desire, we often allow our hurt and pain, preprogrammed scripts, and ego to swoop in and sabotage our good intentions.

We might want victory, but internally we feel the opposite of what we hope for. Our fears, doubts, and insecurities take over, dropping our vibrational state. Mentally we are asking for good things to come to us, but our emotions are sending out wave upon wave of limiting or inhibiting vibrations. Then we are surprised when something unwanted occurs, when things don't work out or end up wondering why we keep creating the same situation.

As they say, *"From your lips to God's ears."* Big or small, God is there, ready to carry out our vibrational requests. When we dwell on positive things, God says, *"Okay,"* and brings them to us. The same holds true when we are consumed by negative thinking. God also says, *"Okay,"* and brings that into our experience as well. He takes everything we think and feel literally and brings us what we ask for.

Galatians 6:7 *says, "For whatsoever a man soweth, that shall he also reap."* This saying implies whatever we send out into the world, be it a vibration, a word, or a deed; it will be returned to us. What we give, so shall we receive. If we hate, we will receive hate. If we love, we will receive love. Criticism only returns criticism, liars will be lied to, and cheaters will be cheated on.

Many of us do not recognize we are focusing on the opposite of our desires. Without conscious awareness of what is happening inside, our wishes, good, bad, or indifferent, will always come true. Why blame God or anyone else when things don't work out?

The real culprit is not our circumstances but our thinking. This is why it is so important to express the highest ideal of ourselves by eliminating or minimizing the negative false images we have created about who and what we are. These negative thoughts only act to bring down our vibration, taking us out of joy and out of alignment.

Dang! It Was Me All Along?

Years ago, I tried organizing in-person classes. I put a lot of effort into developing the curriculum, finding an appropriate location, and advertising the event. I regularly asked for a room filled with students, visualizing a large group of attendees. Then as if on cue, my fears would creep in, and my focus would shift from assuming the room would be packed to, well, the best way I can describe it, internally, I was begging for people to show up. Maybe not a rabbit hole moment, but I would linger in it.

Needless to say, the big day would arrive, and two people would attend. Sometimes no one paid the modest course fee. I gave up trying to organize and promote my own events. I resigned myself to the fact that I could not fill a room, even though I am so cool and smart. In hindsight, I understand that doubt and fear were the predominant energies I was sending out before each big speaking event. I was scared no one would show up and got what I asked for. No one showed up. I can only blame myself and my wanting energy for the results I achieved.

Instant Karma

Oh, and don't worry. We are not instant manifestors. We won't automatically bring into existence whatever happens to be the most active vibration within us. Things do not occur spontaneously in the real world, for the most part. If I am thinking about chocolate cake, it does not wondrously appear in front of me. And needless to say, you also won't be struck by lightning, and the sky won't come falling down on you if you occasionally have a stray negative thought. Our prevailing thoughts determine what is drawn to us. It takes time to shift the predominant narrative and vibration going on inside.

This is not to say that we never manifest in the moment. It can and does happen. We have all had moments when we have experienced 'instant karma.' Usually, we attribute moments of instant karma to when bad things happen to us. We have a mean thought about a person, and we stub our toe on the leg of the coffee table. We can also have positive moments of instant karma. What about those times when you were thinking about buying a new car, a Tesla, and out of the blue, one drives by? Instant karma!

A Soapbox Moment

I have tried to incorporate the teachings of the Law of Attraction into my life for years. I would spend countless hours focusing on attracting new clients or situations which would make me rich and famous. I worked my ass off, thinking my work was divinely inspired, believing it was what I needed to do to get butts in chairs.

I would visualize how many clients I wanted a week. I would do energy work clearing any resistance I had on my calendar. I would send good vibes and intentions out into the universe with a big *"Eat at Joe's"* sign pointing down at me. It seemed to work sometimes, and at other times, it seemed like a complete and utter failure.

With this new round of investigating myself and attempting to heal my inner world, I uncovered extremely helpful guidance coming from experts in this field. Again, my goal is not to make millions of dollars. I just wanted to feel happy, content, and secure.

During my exploration, I detected a deeper component tied to the Law of Attraction which always seemed elusive. The instructors always appeared to tip-toe around what I considered a core puzzle piece. What do I focus on? Do I focus on what I want? Pray for what I want? Beg for what I want, or should my attention be somewhere else?

This is what I discovered. Working with the Law of Attraction is not about focusing on a goal or result. It is all about balancing our energy and keeping it positive and aligned. Staying in alignment and in the flow IS the critical path everyone seems to dance around. Alignment allows spirit to flow readily through us. When we are out of alignment, our system experiences resistance, and then nothing works. Putting too much attention on something and trying hard to make it work can cause it to backfire. You are not projecting good vibes and the highest level of your intentions into the world. You are projecting your fears and doubts, and visions of a potential failure.

A bad day at work can knock you out of alignment. A fight with your kids, troubles with your car, a deal gone wrong, anything that interferes with the flow of spirit through your body inhibits your ability to manifest what you want, not just in one area of your life, but in every area of your life. It all comes down to choosing your thoughts and paying attention to your feelings. It is about deciding on inner peace and quickly recognizing those moments when you have it and when you don't.

I have to say, this insight was a light bulb moment for me. I had to accept the fact that I had been working with these principles wrong all along. No wonder things never worked out the way I wanted. Despite my years of failure, I feel incredibly grateful to now know how to make it work.

Things you desire will begin to emerge when you live in a place of inner tranquility and alignment. Opportunities may appear everywhere around you, or doors may start to open. Pay attention to the insights being offered. And please, please, please, act on the guidance you receive! Follow your spontaneous creative urges, even if they don't make sense. Try not to force the universe into working, let it flow. If you are unsure what to do, ask your higher self, *"What should I be doing now or next?"* Honor the whisperings you perceive, whether it is a thought, a comment from a friend, or something you see on television.

Saying affirmations or making a vision board will not produce the circumstances needed to create what you want. They say God helps those that help themselves. Take the initiative, even if it seems scary and uncomfortable or if your inner critic tries to tell you it will result in a tragic outcome. We might not know why we are being led to do a certain thing, yet in hindsight, we are often glad we did.

One last thing, don't forget to say *"thank you."* Appreciate the things you receive, even if they are less than stellar. Each time you are thankful for something, you tell the universe, *"Please sir, can I have some more?"* This practice opens the door to increasing the blessings in your life. When we ignore the gifts the universe offers us, we are slowing down our energy, decreasing our flow, and making it harder for God to provide.

Weird as this may sound, acknowledge other people's success as well. Why be jealous or resentful of others when things are going well for them? This will only add resistance to your system. Celebrate with them; rejoice in their accomplishments. This will increase your energy flow and raise your vibration even higher.

Final Thought

Without an awareness of our inner world, without knowledge of our prevailing thoughts and scripted emotional responses, we would never be able to recognize what we are projecting out into the world much less fix it. This awareness might also help to explain why our lives seems to work some of the time and less so at others.

Acknowledge when good things seem to happen. Likewise, take the time to evaluate your energy state when challenging events appear in your life. Check inside to see if you were in a positive flow state or if you were engaged in negative thinking. With a bit of luck, it will only takes a few times of having something tragic happen, while realizing you were in a bad emotional place, for you to decide to take steps to change your internal narrative permanently.

People, Not People

"The best kind of people are the ones that come into your life, and make you see the sun where you once saw clouds. The people that believe in your so much, you start to believe in you too. The people that love you, simply for being you. The once in a lifetime kind of people."

— curiano.com

It is much easier to stay aligned when you live alone, secluded on the top of a mountain. It is you and your energy unaffected by the influx of someone else's vibration. Maintaining a balance in your inner world is less problematic when we have fewer energetic distractions. You can experience a certain level of calm without the ups and downs interactions with others can create.

Granted, things happen. We get a flat tire, the dishwasher breaks, and we have to deal with these issues, which can affect our inner being. We can get irritated, cranky, or just plain pissed off. We are human, not saints and having our feathers ruffled periodically is part of life.

For many, this becomes the focus of their attention. They look to these external factors and use them to rate their overall level of happiness. Are things going well, or is my life fraught with issues? One raises our energy while the other diminishes it. An area we overlook, don't think much of, or perhaps go into denial about is our relationships. What happens to our inner world when we connect with others?

In this context, I am not talking exclusively about romantic relationships, which are obviously important, but all of our relationships – friend or foe. We are 'in relationship' with anyone we interact with. This includes the guy who changed our tire, the dishwasher repair man, the people at the supermarket, the dry cleaner, and the representative from the Internal Revenue Service. In any encounter we have, romantic or not, there is an exchange of unseen subtle energies.

We are constantly sending and receiving energy from the world around us. Someone smiles at us as we pass them on the street, compliments how we look or something we have done, our vibration rises. It leaves us feeling good inside. Likewise, when someone intentionally ignores us, criticizes us, shames or guilts us, a surge of troubling thoughts can be activated, leaving us feeling inadequate.

We tend to be more conscious of an energy exchange when interacting personally with someone and less so when talking about what occurs below many people's radars. Would you believe the projected signals we receive can stimulate a subconscious emotional response without a word being said? It is true! Both overt and subtle exchanges can affect our inner world.

The Law Of Resonance

It is believed there are 12 unchanging laws of our universe. These laws are thought to be intrinsic to our lives. The Law of Attraction is one of them. Another one of these laws is the 'Law of Resonance.' The Law of Resonance is one of the reasons the Law of Attraction works, but it also comes into play in the working of our internal state. When we are exposed to someone who shares the same or a similar frequency to our current emotional state, we will spontaneously begin to resonate at a matching vibration.

Let me explain. Everything in nature has a natural frequency, including us. Our predominant or long-standing thoughts and emotions determine our frequency. There are many instances to be found in the natural world regarding the concept of resonance. The classic example is when a middle C tuning fork is struck, other middle C tuning forks will begin to sound while tuning forks calibrated at different frequencies, at notes such as B, G, D, E, or F, lay dormant. The second middle C tuning fork vibrates because it carries a matching resonant frequency to the original.

You can also think of the opera singer, who can cause a wine glass to shatter when hitting a specific note. Why? Because the note she struck matched the resonant frequency of the glass, causing it to vibrate and ultimately break. The same holds true with your radio. The dial on the tuner, 'tunes into' the frequency of the station's broadcast, which is picked up and amplified through your speakers.

The Law of Attraction suggests we connect naturally and harmoniously with people who vibrate at a similar frequency. It feels good, comfortable, to be around them. When our energy drops, we are creating a situation in which we invite people into our experience that will amplify our downward shift, and we will weirdly feel comfortable in their presence. It is all about our vibration.

Baba Ram Dass

Several years ago, I hosted a radio show, *Just Energy Radio*, where I interviewed experts from various fields, including ancient mysteries, health, healing, UFOs, spirituality, and the paranormal. It was a very eclectic mix of alternative thought topics. I was blessed with the opportunity to interview an American spiritual teacher, the guru of modern yoga, Baba Ram Dass.

I had read his seminal book *Be Here Now* when I was in my late teens. To say I was ecstatic to be able to interact with him for a full hour is an understatement. Ram Dass had just released a new book, *Be Love Now: The Path of the Heart*, at the time of our interview.

A few years earlier, from what I had heard, he had suffered a massive stroke and his speech was impaired. I wondered how his challenge would impact the interview. A huge part of me didn't care. I was overjoyed with the notion that I would be able to spend one-on-one time with him, something I never would have dreamed of.

On the day of the show, his people reached out inquiring if I could do the interview via video and not just audio. We were still living in the Stone Age of technology, before podcasts offered video content. Bandwidth-wise, it was implausible, yet anything is possible if you ask spirit and your higher self for a solution. I received the message that I should connect with him on two different computers. I used my regular broadcast computer to host the audio portion of the show and connected with him via video on my laptop.

I can't remember much of what we discussed during our time together. Actually, I don't know if we talked much at all. What I do clearly recall was the high-vibrating, loving energy transmitted from him to me via our video connection. There were long moments of dead air when I would have to say to the listeners, *"I'm sorry, we are just sitting here smiling at each other."* I don't know what experience my listeners were having. I can only hope that what I was feeling was being broadcasted across the airwaves.

I will never forget basking in his infinite loving presence. I'm sharing this story because even though we spoke to each other, his presence greatly affected my energy. He didn't say kind words to me. He just 'was,' and my body moved into resonance with his incredible energy. Even now, years later, I can still feel his high vibration deep within my soul.

Fine-Tuning Our Awareness

Relationships, when discussing the dynamics of our inner world, can be tricky to unwind and understand. There is so much going on, both seen and unseen, that a deeper, direct conversation seems in order. My mission on the outset of this journey was to figure out how to be in a relationship and be happy at the same time. From an internal perspective, what does that look like? How can you have both? So here goes!

There is a level of intimacy we long to experience in all of our relationships. When a relationship is healthy, there is an unspoken commitment to foster each other's growth. We want to feel appreciated, respected, heard, and understood. These uplifting rendezvous set off the release of dopamine and other feel-good hormones in our bodies, leaving us feeling connected.

Healthy individuals thrive on an equal exchange of energy. They are willing to offer the other person their time, attention, and presence. They accept us unconditionally, acknowledging us for who we are, without wanting to change us. These people are real and authentic. They are kind, caring, gentle souls. They do not try to impress us with their greatness. They just are. They plant seeds, offer and invite instead of trying to convince, persuade or manipulate us into their way of thinking. We feel good in their presence.

When we interact with someone who is selfish or indifferent to us, our inner world suffers. One only needs to think of the cold, bureaucratic woman sitting behind the counter at the local governmental office who seemed more interested in going to lunch than helping us. Exchanges with individuals like this can seem cold and distant. They are functional, not loving. There is usually a one-way energy dynamic occurring. We give to them, but they typically offer little in return, including their time or attention. They don't see us, much less appreciate us, unless they want something. We can choose to pay attention to these shifts in our energy and explore them, or we can let them go right over our heads.

Most of us do not live on the top of a mountain. This makes it essential for us to fine-tune our awareness with respect to energy exchanges with others. One crucial factor when dealing with others is our ability to recognize how we traditionally feel. Are you ordinarily calm, cool, and collected throughout the day, or do you find yourself easily triggered or emotionally dysregulated by every cool breeze that passes by? Does worry, fear, restlessness, or anxiety make it challenging to calm down, relax, and center? Notice this. Pay attention to your vibration.

Knowing and recognizing the customary touch and feel of your inner world will make it easier to determine if the people around you are affecting you. Think of a time when you found yourself in a contentious conversation with someone. The desire to win, a sense of competition, or the do-or-die feelings you were experiencing may not have been yours. You could have actually been reflecting the other person's energy causing you to resonate at their lowered level. You can only become aware of this discrepancy in your vibration if you recognize you are not a competitive person in the first place, and the behavior you displayed is unnatural for you.

We don't need to interact with someone to receive their energetic vibration. We have all had the experience of being around someone who has bad mojo, and we automatically feel uncomfortable. It can go deeper than that. Their very presence can awaken a matching emotion, causing one of our core beliefs to be activated.

You are at work and having a great day. You get called into a meeting, and even though nothing untoward occurs, you start to feel nervous. This sets off a cascade of problematic thinking where you find yourself worrying, *"Did I do something wrong?" "Am I in trouble?"* Hopefully, your emerging thoughts are untrue, and in reality, you didn't do anything erroneous. In situations like this, perhaps you unknowingly received the feelings of someone else in the room, which triggered one of your core beliefs and caused you to respond internally.

We often assume the thoughts running through our minds and the feelings we are having in our bodies are ours. We believe these inner sensations are being activated by something we have done or experienced. This is not always the case. The angry, lethargic, backstabbing feelings you have each day at work might not be yours but something you are receiving from your environment.

This concept is not new. For some reason, it is only talked about in certain circles, yet the implication of this dynamic and its impact on us is significant. Learning to recognize when you are being affected by other people's energy can be challenging, but it's not impossible. With a few tricks up your sleeve and an increased awareness of your inner nature, you can learn to decipher your energy from others.

Fighting The Fear

Living through Covid was challenging for everyone. One of its most taxing aspects was dealing with the trepidation tied to the pandemic. *"Will I catch it?" "If I do, will I end up in the hospital and die?" "What about my parents, children, spouse, friends, and family? Will they get it and die too?" "Do I have enough toilet paper to survive this disaster?"*

The intensity of ruinous, catastrophic thoughts that ran through people's minds put many right square into their rabbit holes. Fear ran rampant, and the sheer terror people projected into the world was immeasurable. It was hard not to be affected by the overwhelming dread filling the air.

Not long into the unfolding of these tragic events, and long before the vaccine was available, I became consciously aware of how scared I was feeling. It caused me to stop and evaluate what was going on and inquire if what I was feeling was even mine or if I was unsuspectingly receiving and reacting to what was happening around me.

I began questioning my reality. This is what I surmised. I was not afraid of getting Covid. I eat right and try to take care of myself. I was taking additional supplements to help keep my immune system strong and fend it off or minimize the virus's effect if I did contract it. I believed I would survive even if I did get sick.

With my beliefs in hand and lots of toilet paper, I concluded I wasn't afraid. Okay, maybe a little, but not to the level of discomfort I was experiencing. Once I realized my state was not due to my emotions but came from what I was picking from the people around me, it was easier to manage my alarm. And manage is a great word to use. For a long while, it became my mission to keep myself from getting caught up in the rampant panic that seemed to be everywhere. When I found myself mysteriously triggered, I would ask my higher self, *"Is this me?"*

I would start working with my tools, tapping, breathing, and meditating if the answer was *"No"* in an effort to calm what had been roused. It was hard. Hard to relax. Hard to ground. Hard to stay in alignment. Nevertheless, this simple act of awareness allowed me to work proactively on maintaining an even keel.

There is a vast difference between 'you' being in your body with your feelings versus 'you' in your body with everyone else's feelings mixed in.

Highly sensitive people, the empaths of the world, have to take additional precautions when dealing with their feelings. Empaths are often described as psychic sponges. What doesn't bother many people may affect them significantly. They can be plagued with the reception of broadcasts from others, making separating their thoughts and emotions from those around them even more vital.

Exercise

If you have never tried this, perhaps now would be an excellent time to begin monitoring your inner state around people, your friends, co-workers, and family to see how they feel to you. Do you immediately cross your arms around specific individuals or experience a vague sense of dread or discomfort? Pay attention to this.

Notice the effect this person has on you. Acknowledge any shifts in your energy. Use this new level of discernment to check in on yourself and ask, *"Does this feel good to me?"* You might be surprised by what you discover. Relationships you once thought were good, fun, healing, and high vibrating might not be what you thought they were cracked up to be.

The Dreaded B Word

With your inner assessment in hand, you can use this information to ascertain if a relationship is serving your overall happiness level. We are the only ones who can determine who we allow into our world and who is excluded. This decision, this choice, takes us straight into the realm of creating and maintaining boundaries. We don't need boundaries when we are by ourselves. We just do our thing. Knowing what is acceptable from what is not, what is raising our energy from what is diminishing it, is critical in our interactions with others.

Boundaries have always seemed like a vague and complicated scheme to incorporate into my relationships. You devise some bizarre rule and then have to enforce it, ensuring the other person complies with your request. I could never wrap my mind around this idea, much less impose any. One thing I have learned through my studies is that many people who have boundary issues also suffer from inner wounding. These individuals often struggle with codependency, people-pleasing, and the fawn stress response.

Barry K. Weinhold's book *Breaking Free Of The Codependency Trap*, describes codependency this way. *"Codependency is a feeling disorder. You were taught to ignore your own feelings."* As a child, many discovered the best way to obtain the love and nurturing they desired was to do a good job and take care of their parent's needs first and foremost. This caused the child to deny their feelings and repress/suppress their emotions.

Codependents are often afraid to stand up for themselves because they might lose the other person's love, attention, or affection. They will put on a happy face even when they are hurting inside. They will justify, rationalize and compensate for the feelings they have. This causes them to lie to themselves and unwittingly deceive others to avoid their displeasure.

Their communications are often vague or indirect. This leaves them room to maneuver and dodge any potential bullets. They may, at times, seem as if they have no opinion at all. They will often freeze or offer their pat replies, *"I don't know,"* or *"I don't care,"* when asked what they want. This ensures they don't make the mistake of picking the wrong answer.

This strategy of obtaining approval is often buried so deep within the codependent's core belief system that they do not see their behavior as unhealthy. This is how life is, and cannot imagine any other way of being.

Their lack of an opinion leaves them tolerating hurtful situations with a stiff upper lip, all in an attempt to make things work out. They will mutely endure the discomfort their negative emotions offer rather than rock the ship. Codependent people pleasers often get so wrapped up in the other person's life, focusing all of their attention on the other person's wants, needs, and desires they will willingly discount their own.

I remember countless times when I sensed discordant energy from my partner. They were not happy and had low vibrating energy. Their projection literally felt devastating painful in my body. It didn't take much to overwhelm me and set off a tirade of negative core beliefs. *"Are they upset at me?"* *"Did I do something wrong?"* *"If I did something wrong, what's going to happen?"* I would find myself walking around on eggshells waiting for the other shoe to drop.

I thought the best way of navigating these uncomfortable situations was to soothe their woe, do things to make them smile, and be happy, all in an effort to get them out of their funk and stop projecting bad vibes. If they did communicate what was bothering them, if there were something they wanted or needed, I would obligingly do as they requested. The thought of not complying left me guilt-ridden, yet I often felt resentful when I did as they asked. I rationalized that once they felt better, I would be able to relax and breathe again. It seemed like a better option than feeling awful for days.

I realize now how much I forfeited. I was becoming the person they wanted or needed me to be in order to reduce the tension I was feeling. My sheepish behavior opened the door to me being overlooked, ignored, and taken advantage of. What was I doing wrong? I was not paying attention to my alignment and my happiness. My focus was entirely on them. I never considered inquiring about what I thought or felt or if what was happening was working for me. I also never dared ask for what I wanted. I had zero expectation my request would be granted anyway.

I know I am not alone in this. No one teaches us to check in on ourselves and our level of happiness. We are programmed early on to submit to the whims and dictates of others regardless of how we feel inside. This external focus leaves us compliant and complicit while enabling bad behavior in others.

Here is the crux of having and maintaining boundaries. Boundaries are about adding ourselves to the relationship mix. We bring ourselves into the equation when we ask that one simple mindful question, *"What about me?"* We can use this tiny piece of inner awareness to monitor our emotional state. This question, this 'I Am' type of statement, also allows us to tap into the guidance our soul and higher self provides.

Why Communication Matters

An essential factor in having healthy boundaries includes our ability to communicate. Our relationships often run on autopilot and a series of unspoken agreements. We assume our partner knows what we want and what we are thinking. They are not mind readers any more than we are. The assumptions we make are only stories we tell ourselves about any situation. We only ask for trouble when we create a narrative about someone else.

You can save yourself tons of disappointment if you communicate what you expect. The more precise you are, the better it is. Have the courage to ask questions if their response is vague or you don't fully understand.

Being brave and stating your needs is a much healthier strategy than making assumptions of what they will or will not do or, worse yet, resentfully going along with what they desire. Nothing is more damaging than hanging on to your feelings by stuffing them down and suffering in silence.

We move into a lower energy vibration when we hold on to our thoughts and do not communicate them. Internalizing feelings such as *"I don't want you to treat me this way"* only causes us to send our feelings out to them loud and clear unwittingly. They might not be able to decipher what we are communicating, but they will be able to detect something is going on. This will only enlarge the problem.

I have already shared how my verbal communication skills have been a lifelong challenge. One thing I discovered, as I raised my awareness of my inner world, was whenever I found myself upset, if I could muster up the courage and speak my truth, telling the other person how I felt, the rumination and any inner conflict I was feeling stopped.

The question you have to ask is, *"what's more important, your fear of speaking up or feeling better?"* It takes much more energy to suppress your truth than to speak and act on it. Reflect on how much time you may have spent over the course of your life thinking about a distasteful issue. Too much time will probably be your conclusion.

What you say will be heard and respected without judgment or invalidation if you're dealing with a healthy, high-vibrating person. They will never have you justify how you feel or cause you to fight to have your needs met. They will also not leave you feeling obligated to defend your decision or leave you feeling coerced into explaining why you may feel a certain way.

Traditionally, ego-driven people will offer blowback, get bent out of shape, or walk off in a huff when you identify your needs and set a boundary. This is one way you can tell if a relationship is unhealthy. They may try to convince you that your thoughts and feelings are wrong. They may belittle you, try to manipulate you, threaten you or downright scare you into submission and into alignment with their viewpoint on life. In the end, you might feel worse and wish you never brought the subject up in the first place. This type of behavior is a huge red flag and should be taken seriously.

Wanting Them To Change

Boundaries are not always about protecting us from potential toxic tendencies. We can use them to care for ourselves, where we communicate our preferences. How much have you lost for lack of asking? Let's say you want more attention or nurturing from your partner. You might try to convince yourself you shouldn't or don't need it. But then, one day, you manage to raise the wherewithal to communicate your desire. You might find they wanted increased intimacy also but didn't know how to bring the subject up.

My late husband, Wayne, had an even longer history of toxic, unhealthy romantic relationships. Lying in bed one night early on, I told him I wanted to snuggle. It was as if cuddling were a foreign concept. He shared with me that in any of his multiple marriages, when they went to bed, he would be on one side of the bed and his partner on the other, a gap the size of the Grand Canyon between them. I have to tell you this lack of physical contact wasn't going to work for me. To make a long story short, he tried it and discovered he loved snuggling. Needless to say, the conversation never came up again.

With other individuals, they might begrudgingly meet your needs but are unable to make long-lasting permanent changes.

They might comply briefly to placate your request but will inevitably revert to their old behavior. Think of the alcoholic who stops drinking at his wife's behest. He might abstain for a few weeks but will typically start drinking again. He was not quitting for himself. He stopped because she asked him to. He tried to comply, but ultimately it was not who he was.

Spending time justifying why you want something only lowers your vibration. Trying to talk them into it, arguing your point, and informing them of the errors of their ways reduces your vibration as well. Thinking about the other person's decisions, actions, words, or response also takes you out of the present moment and out of the flow. You are the authority of your feelings. Validate them, whatever they are. Stand by your truth and honor yourself.

This is where the boundary comes into play. Ask for what you want without bashfulness. This tosses the ball squarely into their court. They will hear you and gratefully meet your need, begrudgingly do it, or ignore you completely. People are who they are. They are snugglers or not. For someone who lacks intimacy, getting them to change to satisfy your desire will never become a long-termed behavior on their part.

The question becomes, why be with someone you don't like or who cannot meet your needs? And if they are trying to change you, why be with someone who doesn't enjoy you for you? It is much easier to walk away and find someone more aligned with who you. Asking someone to change is never the answer. You will only continue to experience pain until you recognize and act upon an undeniable truth. They were never really your person.

But I Don't Want To

There are overt and easily understandable reasons why one should have and maintain a boundary. When we experience abuse or maltreatment of any kind, it is a clear sign a boundary needs to be created and maintained. There are also countless things many of us endure to spare someone's feelings. How often have you felt pressured into doing something you didn't want to and then reluctantly did? This is because you didn't have a clear boundary.

More subtly, perhaps you've stayed on the phone longer than you wanted, listening to a friend drone on and on, bored out of your mind. Maybe you've discovered the people around you are constantly depressed, angry, complaining, or in a negative emotional state, yet you haven't done anything to change it. You are lacking a boundary. Maybe a friend only wants to talk about him or herself and appears uninterested in you and your life. Or what about the people who want to decide all the topics of conversation or try to impose their opinion on you while not valuing yours? Again boundaries.

I will bet there have been countless times when you wanted to speak up, hang up, or run away from them. You might leave an uncomfortable encounter feeling like a victim, used and abused. You can stay on the phone and avoid potentially upsetting your friend, or you can decide you have had enough. You can value them, their time, their energy, and their emotions, or you can respect yours.

In her book *Personal Power Through Awareness*, Sandra Roman tells us, *"Unconditional love means keeping your heart open all the time. To do so, you may need to let go of the expectations you have of other people, of wanting then to be anything other than what they are. It means letting go of any need for people to give you things, act in certain ways or respond with love."*

For years, I believed this was the proper and correct way of interacting with others. What a misguided concept. What she doesn't explain is that we have to love and care for ourselves first. We have to be part of the equation. Her ideal of 'unconditional love' caused me to endure all kinds of bad behavior. I was being 'unconditional,' letting them be who they were to my own detriment. Now when unsettling events occur, I am much better about checking in on myself and putting a quick end to things if necessary.

You are not valuing yourself when you experience unpleasant or disagreeable feelings at the hand of another. I'm afraid to say this, but the pain you may sense could be self-inflicted. You are allowing it to happen. You've let their happiness be more important to you than your own. When we stay in relationships that are not in alignment with our soul's desire, we are only punishing ourselves. We are also sending the other person the message they do not have to honor or respect us either.

Loving someone does not mean their feelings are more important than ours, or their rights are more significant and should be considered first. Who we are and what we want is important and has value too. Boundaries ensure we are listening to ourselves and acting on our feelings. They allow us to give our needs the same status we may have been giving others for years.

Why walk around feeling unloved, depleted, angry, depressed, or drained? Getting clear on your boundaries lets you live your life feeling whole, congruent, happy, and fulfilled. It might seem selfish or even narcissistic when you put yourself ahead of others, but it is a very loving act. You are loving yourself. You are prioritizing yourself, your happiness, and your well-being. And we can only create boundaries when we pay attention and honor what is happening inside.

Purgatory

Once a request is stated, the other person has the right to say no. Having someone deny one of our wishes can, without a doubt, diminish our energy. A *"no"* is always hard to hear. Sometimes we have to accept their response unconditionally and move on. Then there are times when their refusal is something we need to take a closer look at.

What we share may be vitally important to our well-being and us. An approach I employ when my requests are dismissed and my energy drops is to put the other person in 'purgatory.' Purgatory is like the penalty box ice hockey player go to when they commit an offense. Mentally, this image lets me put them 'over there.' It allows me to observe them and their behaviors detached from my emotions. I love the whole concept of purgatory.

It is one thing to have a fight or misunderstanding and have the flow of our energy become misaligned. It happens to all of us, even in our closest relationships. People who consistently offer us an outright *"no"* or ignore what we ask for should spend time in purgatory. We can use this emotional and energetic break to decide what to do next.

The injurious thing would be to ignore their behavior, dismiss our needs, and go on as if nothing happened. This will only cause us to hurt ourselves. Toss them in purgatory, especially if you are unsure of your feelings. Take a step back. Observe them or the situation. Check-in to see if one of your core beliefs has been triggered or if your downward energy shift indicates you have begun resonating with their lower vibration.

Apply a consequence if you feel it is appropriate. You might decide to talk to them and clarify your request, or you may feel it is more suited to reduce the time you spend with them. Ask your higher self what your best course of action should be. And if you hurt their feelings, please don't feel guilty. You are not responsible for their emotions, only yours.

Sometimes people will keep pushing our boundaries. You may have to get tougher with these individuals, the consequences more extreme. There can be hard, brutal, yet honest facts we have to be willing to face. Situations may arise when we are better served to let a person leave our experience rather than having them hang around with our inner world in constant ruins. Ask yourself *"why am I sticking around if I spend more time in their presence feeling unhappy?"* Why have your vibration consistently lowered when you can use your energy for better things, like yourself?

I know this sounds harsh, but again, it is a very loving act. Walking away may hurt for a while, but you will heal. Acting on your inner guidance is a sign of strength, not failure. Think of it as a gift you are giving yourself. Reflect on how much emotional pain and suffering you may be saving yourself in the long run. This is especially true if there is an ongoing pattern of minimizing or dismissing your needs. And if they walk away, thank God. Revel in your freedom as the door hits them in the ass.

Emotional Neutrality

It is near impossible to decipher our inner truth when our emotions are flared. It can be even trickier to realign our energy in someone else's presence when there is a direct connection between the two of you. It might also seem strange if you close your eyes, start breathing deeply, or commence a round of tapping while you are in the middle of a conversation. If you are struggling to sort things out and shift your vibration to a higher one, an excellent tactic is to excuse yourself from the prickly interaction. Leave the room or hang up the phone.

It is better to take a quick trip to the restroom to calm down and become more present then continue on with your emotions in a tizzy. Break out your tools and focus on yourself. Do anything that will help discharge the discordant energy you are feeling, especially if you are flustered. There may also be times when a brief mindfulness moment is not enough. It is perfectly reasonable to tell the other person you would like to come back and continue the discussion later. It might be a prudent to refer to the mindfulness question on page 87, *Working Through An Issue*, to help you gain clarity on what is going on and what you are feeling.

Keep the time between an uncomfortable situation, such as a boundary violation, and the follow-up communication as short as possible. When you return, try to engage the other person from a place of 'neutrality.' When interacting from a neutral position, we communicate from a place of purpose, not emotions. We are disconnected from our preprogrammed reflexive positioning, which is never productive.

It is easier to share our deepest truths in a loving way when we are neutral, in alignment, and tuned into our divine souls. It invites the other person to participate in the encounter with honest curiosity, where they will feel appreciated, validated, encouraged, and nurtured. We are likewise more apt to listen to them without becoming upset or being overrun by the judgments of our egos. Often when we approach another individual in the energy of neutrality, they will naturally begin to resonate at this higher frequency. This is when a frank, honest discussion can occur.

If you find yourself starting to become defensive, wanting to express anger, or as if you have to defend yourself, don't be provoked. Back away instead. Don't get caught up in their desire for confrontation. This will only cause you to match their vibration, and what you say or how you react might not come from a place of compassion but from your triggered egoic mind.

Worst case scenario, you can always fall back and move the conversion to the phone or text messaging, especially when dealing with combative individuals. This physical separation can help you to maintain your inner world and support you as you endeavor to say what you have to say without being overpowered by their hostile vibration. Communicating this way might not be the best solution, but it is better than suppressing your inner truth.

Also, don't lose track of your feelings by focusing too much on theirs or allowing their words or behaviors to take you out of alignment. Decide what you want to do, what is in your best interest or highest good, and keep your focus on that. Matching their low-level vibration and falling into their way of thinking can only lead to an unsatisfactory relationship and a miserable life for you.

One final thought before we move on. Anyone who can maintain a neutral stance with loved ones in the face of another's anger and pain should congratulate themselves. They have mastered one of the most challenging lessons in staying in alignment.

Final Thoughts

No man is an island. We cannot avoid relationships but we can manage who we allow into our lives and for how long. Sometimes we cannot avoid dealing with less than pleasurable people who mess with our energy. Toss them back, put them in purgatory, or simply be grateful the encounter ended.

For those looking for love, tuning into your emotions and attending to your inner world allows you to separate the wheat from the chaff. Hold your space and keep our energy high when interacting with others. Look inside and ask yourself *"what about me?"* if you detect a downward shift. Love, honor and respect yourself by following the guidance you receive by taking inspired action.

If things don't work out, dwelling on a relationship isn't the answer. This behavior also causes you to stay in a lower vibrating energy longer than necessary. It keeps you from having what you most want, to feel happy inside. Take time to reflect on the relationship after all is said and done. Ask your higher self, *"What did I learn from this?"*

Sometimes the benefits we gain are painful to hear. When we take the time to assess where we have been, what role we played, or what harmful preprogrammed scripts were activated, we expand ourselves into a new level of being. This helps us learn and grow with the possibility of transforming our bad habits into healthier ones that better serve us. Find gratitude for the lessons you learned.

Stick with the people who leave your vibration high, with you feeling good inside, and your alignment intact. They are the keepers! Let the rest go. You'll be happy you did.

Final, Final Thoughts

"Nobody can go back and start a new beginning, but anyone can start today and make a new ending."
- Maria Robinson

My journey with you is at its end. One last thing before I go. I can only hope my words, the concept explored, and the exercises provided have ignited the desire to change. Very few people put a priority on having a joyous inner world. We often pray, breathe, tap, meditate, or clean our houses when our lives are in the crapper. We pull our tools out of the drawer, dust them off, expecting them to work, and then get frustrated when we don't find relief.

Have increased awareness become part of who you are and how you interact with the world daily. Focusing on your inner world is a forever thing. It is like dieting. You lose 100 pounds. If you return to your old food routines once your weight goal is achieved, the net result is you will more than likely put the excess weight back on. The same holds true here. Do you want to return to the way you were living before - on autopilot?

By taking a moment to breathe every day, reflect, and become more mindful of your inner state, these new behaviors will quickly become second nature. In time, you will not have to constantly remind yourself to practice. It will happen automatically. *"We are what we practice,"* writer Avram Davis observed. *"If we become angry a lot, then essentially we are practicing anger. And we get quite good at it. Conversely, if we practice being joyful, then a joyful person is what we become."*

Since the ending of my last relationship, I have actively worked on raising my awareness to the activities of my inner world. I didn't just focus on one area of my life. I focused on everything going on inside. I wanted to learn how I operated and uncovered that I was a mess. I started this voyage as a chronic ruminator with a deep-seated fear of financial ruin. I allowed my ego to rule and stories of impending disaster to take on a life of their own. This kept me running and running, trying to make things happen in order to achieve the elusive brass ring.

I cannot tell you how researching this topic has been a lifesaver. I literally have a library full of books I thought would help me overcome myself. I eagerly read these titles, anticipating a grand metamorphosis. Regretfully, that never happened. I did become really smart, but the pain and anxiety I constantly felt never diminished.

All of that changed when I started exploring mindfulness and mindful awareness precepts. I discovered it was impossible to stop the negative chatter going on inside, and be in the present moment, without doing something to get me there, especially when a trigger was activated. I never connected the dots between the tools I had at my disposal and using them to create a happier life.

It was hard to meditate, hard to ground, hard to do anything to restore my sense of balance when it felt chaotic inside. In hindsight, I can see now I only focused on what was happening inside when things became intolerable, if at all. And then nothing worked.

My studies led me to a series of new tools that I could use to calm the beast inside. I found them simple to use and easy to deploy. Many of these practices are represented in this book. I didn't randomly decide to include them. I lived them, put them through their paces, and they've never failed me.

I began noticing things shifting, getting easier not long after starting this practice. My distaste for feeling bad, upset, angry, frustrated, or scared spurred me on to pay attention even more. Even on days when I would find myself feeling really irritable, I reveled in the moments when I experienced a little relief. In a short time, I didn't have to constantly remind myself to breathe, do a round of tapping, or 17-second rule something when I felt my energy shift. These habits were becoming part of my life.

With my never-ending toxic thoughts on the back burner, I realized I was calmer and progressively more centered in my emotional space. I was spending more time feeling peaceful and content inside. Life is so much better than it used to be. I no longer walk around fearful or stressed, filled with an *"I've got to get this done, or I will die"* energy in the forefront.

Surprisingly, my monetary situation also improved while somehow doing less work. It is a mystery and will attribute it to the Law of Attraction at work. Granted, I, like everyone on this planet, am a work in progress, yet all I can say is, *"Thank you!"*

How Can You Tell You Have Arrived

I am often asked, *"How do I know if I am heading in the right direction?"* You may detect things changing. The changes may seem subtle at first. You may only be able to focus your mind for a few seconds at first. You might notice how much your brain races as your body relaxes and you become increasingly mindful of your inner world. These thoughts aren't new. They were merely occurring in the background, flying under the radar of your conscious mind. Your ability to remain in the present moment will linger as you increasingly focus on being in the 'Now.' The more you practice, the longer you will be able to remain.

You will have good thought days and bad thought days. You will have days when you are running on autopilot and days when you are a conscious participant in your life. If you are having a bad day, cut yourself some slack. It is a process. Celebrate your good days, your happy moments, and the periods when you are feeling calm and peaceful. In the same way, rejoice the downright awful days. We learn and grow the most through our failures, our missed opportunities, and our disappointments.

Finding it takes you less time, energy, or preparation to get yourself back into the flow is another sign. Life could seem more manageable, or you might experience fewer struggles and more acceptance. You could be more patient in your encounters with others, with fewer onboard assumptions. A general feeling of being increasingly connected to the world around you may emerge. This is also a sign of improvement.

You may also take a keen interest in what is happening inside, spending more time seeking the guidance of your upper soul instead of worldly pleasures. You could find yourself being drawn to learn all you can to facilitate increased feelings of calmness. You may see yourself going in a different direction from others, where you are valuing yourself over accepting their choices. These are all indicators you are moving up the soul ladder and actively engaging in the healing process.

One day you might wake up and think, *"Life is good."* There might be a strange absence of negative thoughts, rumination, or worry. You might feel calm, connected, joyful, relaxed, and not neurotic. You might look out the window and realize it is a beautiful day. You may feel satisfied with yourself and your achievements. You could even discover you are at peace with yourself and that life is worth living.

Happiness isn't about the things we have in life. Being happy is all about the alignment of our energy. All we need to do is pay attention to what makes us feel good, feel whole. Our primary goal, our first priority to living peacefully, should always be to focus on what we are feeling. Make this your habit, your practice, your mission in life. Not every now and then, but moment by moment. Wouldn't that be a blessing?

By choosing the path of joy, you will feel better, happier, more confident, and more secure more of the time. And even if clouds form and a storm rolls through, your ability to navigate it without the emotional ups and downs you may have experienced in the past will seem diminished. So revel in your failures just as much as you revel in your successes. Keep your attention focused inward and upward. By doing this, you can create life you have been dreaming of.

About Rita Louise, PhD

A gifted and talented clairvoyant medical intuitive, Dr. Rita Louise helps people identify the root causes of their concerns. She is a Naturopathic physician and the founder of the Institute Of Applied Energetics that trains students in the art of medical intuition, intuitive counseling, and energy medicine.

She is the author of the books *The Dysfunctional Dance Of The Empath And Narcissist, Stepping Out Of Eden, ET Chronicles: What Myth And Legend Have To Say About Human Origin, Avoiding The Cosmic 2X4, Dark Angels: An Insider's Guide To Ghosts, Spirits & Attached Entities* and *The Power Within*. She is also the producer of a number of feature length as well as video shorts.

Dr. Louise credits early childhood influences for the direction her life would take. By the age of 8, she developed a deep interest in ancient traditions, culture, archaeology and human origins. As time went on, she began searching for spiritual self-discovery pursuing topics including health and wellness, philosophy and the esoteric arts and sciences.

Dr. Louise graduated San Jose State University with a degree in Industrial Design and worked as an electro-mechanical designer and Engineering Services Manager in the military industrial complex. She is a graduate of the Berkeley Psychic Institute where she studied meditation, energy medicine, and learned how to perform clairvoyant readings. After establishing a private practice, Dr. Louise returned to school full time, earning a degree as a Naturopath and a Ph.D. in Natural Health Counseling.

A frequent consultant to the media, Dr. Louise has appeared on television and film and has mystified listeners during her countless radio interviews. Dr. Louise has appeared as a keynote speaker at hundreds of events around the country where she has spoken on topics such as relationships, ancient mysteries, mythology, ancient aliens, intuition, ghosts and the paranormal. Her countless writings have appeared in books, magazines and newsletters around the world.

Her webpage is SoulHealer.com.

The Dysfunctional Dance Of The Empath And Narcissist

ISBN # 978-0975864951

When people enter into a new relationship, they do not go looking for the rotten apple at the bottom of the barrel. However, countless individuals repeatedly find themselves in these hurtful situations and do not understand why. A recent Facebook survey of people who self-identify as being empathic revealed a startling insight. Over 80% of the 1,300 respondents disclosed they had suffered from some form of abuse or neglect during their childhood.

Dr. Rita Louise's recent book *The Dysfunctional Dance Of The Empath And Narcissist* digs deep into this issue. It takes an in-depth look at the dynamics between the loving, compassionate, and often selfless empaths and those willing to take from them, the self-serving narcissists, and endeavors to uncover the unconscious patterns that keep them trapped in cycles of abusive, toxic relationships.

Regardless of what happened to a person when they were young, they have the power to redefine themselves and their life. It is possible to break free of these destructive, negative patterns and finally experience the loving, healthy relationship they have always desired.

"This book is packed with lots of powerful, insightful information that will lead one to a better understanding of themselves and how to become the magnetic embodiment of the relationship one truly seeks."

- Keith Anthony Blanchard
Spiritual Teacher and host of Center of Light Radio

www.ingramcontent.com/pod-product-compliance
Lightning Source LLC
Chambersburg PA
CBHW071906290426
44110CB00013B/1297